Interactive Notebooks
LANGUAGE ARTS

Grade 6

Credits

Author: Pamela Walker McKenzie
Content Editors: Elise Craver, Chris Schwab, Angela Triplett

Visit *carsondellosa.com* for correlations to Common Core, state, national, and Canadian provincial standards.

Carson-Dellosa Publishing, LLC
PO Box 35665
Greensboro, NC 27425 USA
carsondellosa.com

978-1-4838-3129-9
01-341157784

Table of Contents

© Carson-Dellosa • CD-104913

What Are Interactive Notebooks?

Interactive notebooks are a unique form of note taking. Teachers guide students through creating pages of notes on new topics. Instead of being in the traditional linear, handwritten format, notes are colorful and spread across the pages. Notes also often include drawings, diagrams, and 3-D elements to make the material understandable and relevant. Students are encouraged to complete their notebook pages in ways that make sense to them. With this personalization, no two pages are exactly the same.

Because of their creative nature, interactive notebooks allow students to be active participants in their own learning. Teachers can easily differentiate pages to address the levels and needs of each learner. The notebooks are arranged sequentially, and students can create tables of contents as they create pages, making it simple for students to use their notebooks for reference throughout the year. The interactive, easily personalized format makes interactive notebooks ideal for engaging students in learning new concepts.

Using interactive notebooks can take as much or as little time as you like. Students will initially take longer to create pages but will get faster as they become familiar with the process of creating pages. You may choose to only create a notebook page as a class at the beginning of each unit, or you may choose to create a new page for each topic within a unit. You can decide what works best for your students and schedule.

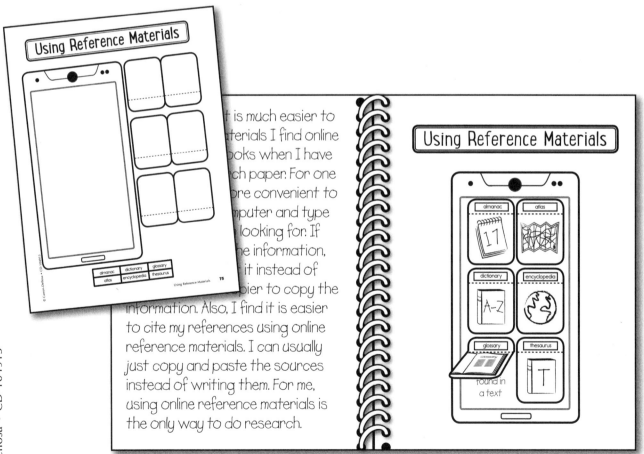

A student's interactive notebook for using reference materials

Getting Started

You can start using interactive notebooks at any point in the school year. Use the following guidelines to help you get started in your classroom. (For more specific details, management ideas, and tips, see page 10.)

1. Plan each notebook.

Use the planning template (page 9) to lay out a general plan for the topics you plan to cover in each notebook for the year.

2. Choose a notebook type.

Interactive notebooks are usually either single-subject, spiral-bound notebooks, composition books, or three-ring binders with loose-leaf paper. Each type presents pros and cons. See page 5 for a more in-depth look at each type of notebook.

3. Allow students to personalize their notebooks.

Have students decorate their notebook covers, as well as add their names and subjects. This provides a sense of ownership and emphasizes the personalized nature of the notebooks.

4. Number the pages and create the table of contents.

Have students number the bottom outside corner of each page, front and back. When completing a new page, adding a table of contents entry will be easy. Have students title the first page of each notebook "Table of Contents." Have them leave several blank pages at the front of each notebook for the table of contents. Refer to your general plan for an idea of about how many entries students will be creating.

5. Start creating pages.

Always begin a new page by adding an entry to the table of contents. Create the first notebook pages along with students to model proper format and expectations.

This book contains individual topics for you to introduce. Use the pages in the order that best fits your curriculum. You may also choose to alter the content presented to better match your school's curriculum. The provided lesson plans often do not instruct students to add color. Students should make their own choices about personalizing the content in ways that make sense to them. Encourage students to highlight and color the pages as they desire while creating them.

After introducing topics, you may choose to add more practice pages. Use the reproducibles (pages 78–96) to easily create new notebook pages for practice or to introduce topics not addressed in this book.

Use the grading rubric (page 11) to grade students' interactive notebooks at various points throughout the year. Provide students copies of the rubric to glue into their notebooks and refer to as they create pages.

What Type of Notebook Should I Use?

Spiral Notebook

The pages in this book are formatted for a standard one-subject notebook.

Pros

- Notebook can be folded in half.
- Page size is larger.
- It is inexpensive.
- It often comes with pockets for storing materials.

Cons

- Pages can easily fall out.
- Spirals can snag or become misshapen.
- Page count and size vary widely.
- It is not as durable as a binder.

Tips

- Encase the spiral in duct tape to make it more durable.
- Keep the notebooks in a central place to prevent them from getting damaged in desks.

Composition Notebook

Pros

- Pages don't easily fall out.
- Page size and page count are standard.
- It is inexpensive.

Cons

- Notebook cannot be folded in half.
- Page size is smaller.
- It is not as durable as a binder.

Tips

- Copy pages meant for standard-sized notebooks at 85 or 90 percent. Test to see which works better for your notebook.

Binder with Loose-Leaf Paper

Pros

- Pages can be easily added, moved, or removed.
- Pages can be removed individually for grading.
- You can add full-page printed handouts.
- It has durable covers.

Cons

- Pages can easily fall out.
- Pages aren't durable.
- It is more expensive than a notebook.
- Students can easily misplace or lose pages.
- Larger size makes it more difficult to store.

Tips

- Provide hole reinforcers for damaged pages.

How to Organize an Interactive Notebook

You may organize an interactive notebook in many different ways. You may choose to organize it by unit and work sequentially through the book. Or, you may choose to create different sections that you will revisit and add to throughout the year. Choose the format that works best for your students and subject.

An interactive notebook includes different types of pages in addition to the pages students create. Non-content pages you may want to add include the following:

Title Page

This page is useful for quickly identifying notebooks. It is especially helpful in classrooms that use multiple interactive notebooks for different subjects. Have students write the subject (such as "Language Arts") on the title page of each interactive notebook. They should also include their full names. You may choose to have them include other information such as the teacher's name, classroom number, or class period.

Table of Contents

The table of contents is an integral part of the interactive notebook. It makes referencing previously created pages quick and easy for students. Make sure that students leave several pages at the beginning of each notebook for a table of contents.

Expectations and Grading Rubric

It is helpful for each student to have a copy of the expectations for creating interactive notebook pages. You may choose to include a list of expectations for parents and students to sign, as well as a grading rubric (page 11).

Unit Title Pages

Consider using a single page at the beginning of each section to separate it. Title the page with the unit name. Add a tab (page 78) to the edge of the page to make it easy to flip to the unit. Add a table of contents for only the pages in that unit.

Glossary

Reserve a six-page section at the back of the notebook where students can create a glossary. Draw a line to split in half the front and back of each page, creating 24 sections. Combine Q and R and Y and Z to fit the entire alphabet. Have students add an entry as each new vocabulary word is introduced.

Formatting Student Notebook Pages

The other major consideration for planning an interactive notebook is how to treat the left and right sides of a notebook spread. Interactive journals are usually viewed with the notebook open flat. This creates a left side and a right side. You have several options for how to treat the two sides of the spread.

Traditionally, the right side is used for the teacher-directed part of the lesson, and the left side is used for students to interact with the lesson content. The lessons in this book use this format. However, you may prefer to switch the order for your class so that the teacher-directed learning is on the left and the student input is on the right.

It can also be important to include standards, learning objectives, or essential questions in interactive notebooks. You may choose to write these on the top-left side of each page before completing the teacher-directed page on the right side. You may also choose to have students include the "Introduction" part of each lesson in that same top-left section. This is the *in, through, out* method. Students enter *in* the lesson on the top left of the page, go *through* the lesson on the right page, and exit *out* of the lesson on the bottom left with a reflection activity.

The following chart details different types of items and activities that you could include on each side.

Left Side Student Output	Right Side Teacher-Directed Learning
• learning objectives • essential questions • I Can statements • brainstorming • making connections • summarizing • making conclusions • practice problems • opinions • questions • mnemonics • drawings and diagrams	• vocabulary and definitions • mini-lessons • folding activities • steps in a process • example problems • notes • diagrams • graphic organizers • hints and tips • big ideas

Planning for the Year

Making a general plan for interactive notebooks will help with planning, grading, and testing throughout the year. You do not need to plan every single page, but knowing what topics you will cover and in what order can be helpful in many ways.

Use the Interactive Notebook Plan (page 9) to plan your units and topics and where they should be placed in the notebooks. Remember to include enough pages at the beginning for the non-content pages, such as the title page, table of contents, and grading rubric. You may also want to leave a page at the beginning of each unit to place a mini table of contents for just that section.

In addition, when planning new pages, it can be helpful to sketch the pieces you will need to create. Use the following notebook template and notes to plan new pages.

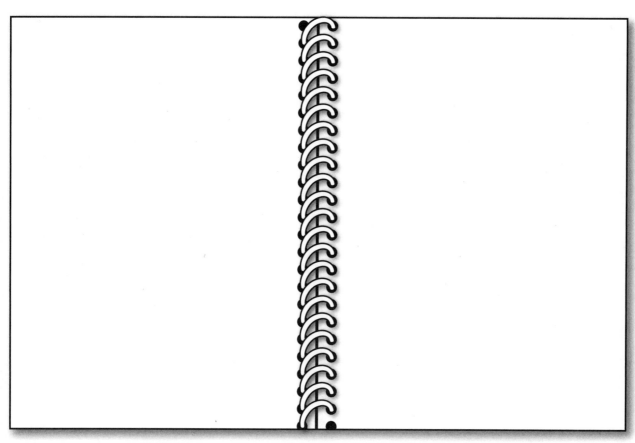

Left Side   **Right Side**

Notes

_____

_____

_____

Interactive Notebook Plan

Page	Topic	Page	Topic
1		51	
2		52	
3		53	
4		54	
5		55	
6		56	
7		57	
8		58	
9		59	
10		60	
11		61	
12		62	
13		63	
14		64	
15		65	
16		66	
17		67	
18		68	
19		69	
20		70	
21		71	
22		72	
23		73	
24		74	
25		75	
26		76	
27		77	
28		78	
29		79	
30		80	
31		81	
32		82	
33		83	
34		84	
35		85	
36		86	
37		87	
38		88	
39		89	
40		90	
41		91	
42		92	
43		93	
44		94	
45		95	
46		96	
47		97	
48		98	
49		99	
50		100	

Managing Interactive Notebooks in the Classroom

Working with Younger Students

- Use your yearly plan to preprogram a table of contents that you can copy and give to students to glue into their notebooks, instead of writing individual entries.

- Have assistants or parent volunteers precut pieces.

- Create glue sponges to make gluing easier. Place large sponges in plastic containers with white glue. The sponges will absorb the glue. Students can wipe the backs of pieces across the sponges to apply the glue with less mess.

Creating Notebook Pages

- For storing loose pieces, add a pocket to the inside back cover. Use the envelope pattern (page 81), an envelope, a jumbo library pocket, or a resealable plastic bag. Or, tape the bottom and side edges of the two last pages of the notebook together to create a large pocket.

- When writing under flaps, have students trace the outline of each flap so that they can visualize the writing boundary.

- Where the dashed line will be hidden on the inside of the fold, have students first fold the piece in the opposite direction so that they can see the dashed line. Then, students should fold the piece back the other way along the same fold line to create the fold in the correct direction.

- To avoid losing pieces, have students keep all of their scraps on their desks until they have finished each page.

- To contain paper scraps and avoid multiple trips to the trash can, provide small groups with small buckets or tubs.

- For students who run out of room, keep full and half sheets available. Students can glue these to the bottom of the pages and fold them up when not in use.

Dealing with Absences

- Create a model notebook for absent students to reference when they return to school.

- Have students cut a second set of pieces as they work on their own pages.

Using the Notebook

- To organize sections of the notebook, provide each student with a sheet of tabs (page 78).

- To easily find the next blank page, either cut off the top-right corner of each page as it is used or attach a long piece of yarn or ribbon to the back cover to be used as a bookmark.

Interactive Notebook Grading Rubric

4

_____ Table of contents is complete.

_____ All notebook pages are included.

_____ All notebook pages are complete.

_____ Notebook pages are neat and organized.

_____ Information is correct.

_____ Pages show personalization, evidence of learning, and original ideas.

3

_____ Table of contents is mostly complete.

_____ One notebook page is missing.

_____ Notebook pages are mostly complete.

_____ Notebook pages are mostly neat and organized.

_____ Information is mostly correct.

_____ Pages show some personalization, evidence of learning, and original ideas.

2

_____ Table of contents is missing a few entries.

_____ A few notebook pages are missing.

_____ A few notebook pages are incomplete.

_____ Notebook pages are somewhat messy and unorganized.

_____ Information has several errors.

_____ Pages show little personalization, evidence of learning, or original ideas.

1

_____ Table of contents is incomplete.

_____ Many notebook pages are missing.

_____ Many notebook pages are incomplete.

_____ Notebook pages are too messy and unorganized to use.

_____ Information is incorrect.

_____ Pages show no personalization, evidence of learning, or original ideas.

Interacting with Text

Introduction

Before class, bring in or make copies of the backs of several cereal boxes so that each pair of students will have one. Instruct students to make a list of things they should think about or do before, during, and after reading the cereal boxes in order to get the deepest meaning possible. For example, having them recall a time they've eaten this cereal before or a similar cereal. Then, ask partners to read the boxes and discuss the text. Point out that interacting with text gives readers a deeper understanding of what they read.

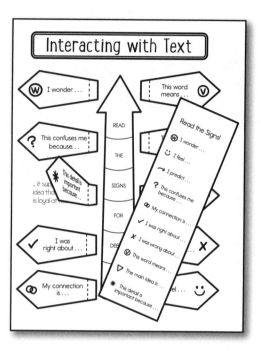

Creating the Notebook Page

Guide students through the following steps to complete the right-hand page in their notebooks.

1. Add a Table of Contents entry for the Interacting with Text pages.

2. Cut out the title and glue it to the top of the page.

3. Cut out the *READ THE SIGNS* arrow piece and glue it to the center of the page below the title.

4. Cut out the sign flaps. Apply glue to the back of the left or right section of each piece and attach five flaps to each side of the arrow.

5. Discuss each symbol and phrase and how to use each symbol to interact with the text during reading. Under each flap, write an example from a current text you are reading.

6. Cut out the *Read the Signs!* bookmark. Glue it to a piece of construction paper for durability and keep it in the book you are currently reading. Use it as a reference when making notes in your interactive reading journal.

Reflect on Learning

To complete the left-hand page, have students elaborate on each of the symbols and thinking stems. Students should write about when each symbol and thinking stem might be used and why it would be helpful for readers to use them as they read.

Interacting with Text

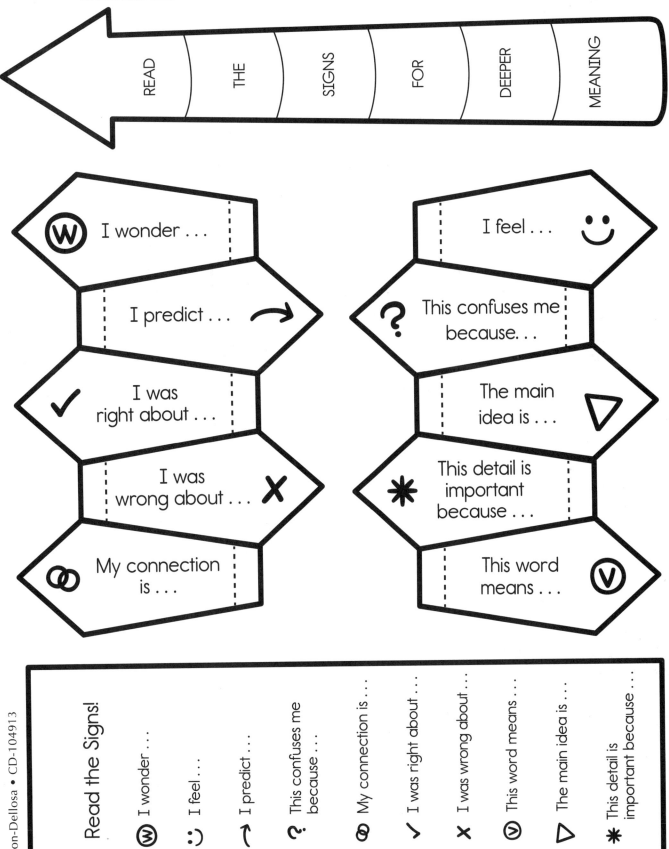

READ · THE · SIGNS · FOR · DEEPER · MEANING

W — I wonder . . .

I predict . . .

✓ — I was right about . . .

✗ — I was wrong about . . .

∞ — My connection is . . .

I feel . . . ☺

? — This confuses me because. . .

The main idea is . . . ▷

∗ — This detail is important because . . .

This word means . . . Ⓥ

Read the Signs!

Ⓦ I wonder . . .

:) I feel . . .

↑ I predict . . .

↶ This confuses me because . . .

∞ My connection is . . .

✓ I was right about . . .

✗ I was wrong about . . .

Ⓥ This word means . . .

▷ The main idea is . . .

∗ This detail is important because . . .

Citing Text Evidence

Introduction

Tell students that two people just read the same article about why their town should build a skate park. Then, write the following on the board: *Jack: I agree with the author because our town really needs a skate park. Chris: I agree with the author because he included a poll showing that 63% of residents feel a skate park would have a positive effect on our town.* Discuss how all readers have ideas about what they read. Point out that Jack and Chris have the same opinion. Have students discuss who would be taken more seriously in a discussion on this topic and why.

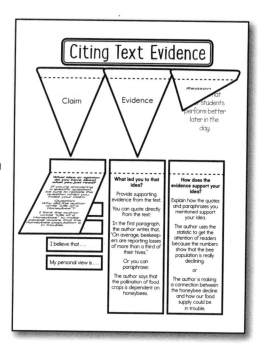

Creating the Notebook Page

Guide students through the following steps to complete the right-hand page in their notebooks.

1. Add a Table of Contents entry for the Citing Text Evidence pages.

2. Cut out the title and glue it to the top of the page.

3. Cut out the *Claim, Evidence,* and *Reason* flaps. Apply glue to the back of the top section of each piece and attach them below the title in the following order: *Claim, Evidence, Reason.*

4. Cut out the *What idea . . . , What led you . . . ,* and *How does the evidence . . .* flaps. Apply glue to the back of the top section of each piece and attach them below the correct pennant.

5. Cut out the sentence starter labels. Discuss whether each sentence starter is appropriate for making a claim, providing evidence, or explaining reasoning. Glue each under the correct *What idea . . . , What led you . . . ,* or *How does the evidence . . .* flaps.

6. Under the *Claim, Evidence,* and *Reason* flaps, write about a text you are currently reading. Under *Claim,* state an idea you have about the text. Under *Evidence,* cite text evidence to support your idea. Under *Reason,* explain your reason.

Reflect on Learning

To complete the left-hand page, have students use the notes they wrote under the *Claim, Evidence,* and *Reason* flaps to write a paragraph that shares their ideas about a text they are reading.

Answer Key
What idea . . . you just read?: I think that, My opinion is, I believe that, My personal view is; What led you . . . idea?: The author explains that, In the first paragraph, the text states, The author defines, The author describes; How does the evidence . . . idea?: This evidence shows that, This illustrates that, This statistic highlights that, The author included this to show

Citing Text Evidence

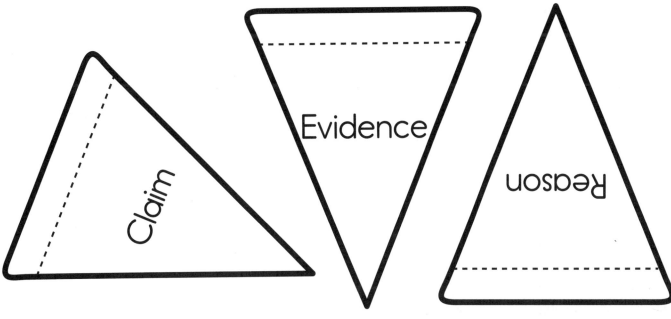

Claim

Evidence

Reason

What idea or opinion do you have about what you just read?	What led you to that idea?	How does the evidence support your idea?
If you're answering a specific question, be sure to restate the question when you make your claim.	Provide supporting evidence from the text.	Explain how the quotes and paraphrases you mentioned support your idea.
Question: Why did the author write "Life of a Honeybee"?	You can quote directly from the text:	The author uses the statistic to get the attention of readers because the numbers show that the bee population is really declining.
I think the author wrote "Life of a Honeybee" to make people aware that the honeybee population is in trouble.	In the first paragraph, the author writes that, "On average, beekeepers are reporting losses of more than a third of their hives."	or
	Or you can paraphrase:	The author is making a connection between the honeybee decline and how our food supply may be in trouble.
	The author says that the pollination of food crops is dependent on honeybees.	

I think that . . .	In the first paragraph, the text states . . .	This statistic highlights that . . .
The author explains that . . .	My opinion is . . .	The author included this to show . . . .
This evidence shows that	The author describes	I believe that . . .
This illustrates that . . .	My personal view is . . .	The author defines . . .

Author's Purpose

Introduction

Remind students that the three main reasons authors write are to persuade, to inform, or to entertain. Present students with the following excerpts and ask them to determine the author's purpose for each. 1) "With more honeybee colonies collapsing each year, we are at the point where we must make changes before it's too late." 2) "In a bee colony, the queen's only job is to lay eggs." 3) "Queen Bee gathered her royal warriors around her and gave the order to attack!" Have students label each excerpt with a purpose, and then discuss how they were able to determine the author's purpose for each excerpt.

Creating the Notebook Page

Guide students through the following steps to complete the right-hand page in their notebooks.

1. Add a Table of Contents entry for the Author's Purpose pages.

2. Cut out the title and glue it to the top of the page.

3. Cut out the author's picture and glue it to the bottom of the page.

4. Cut out the idea cloud flaps. Apply glue to the back of the left sections and attach them to the page above the author's head.

5. Discuss each of the ideas the author is considering. How are they alike? How are they different? What does the author want to accomplish with each of her ideas?

6. Cut out the *inform*, *persuade*, and *entertain* labels. Read the ideas on the flaps and glue the correct author's purpose label under each flap.

Reflect on Learning

To complete the left-hand page, have students write three different ideas for written pieces that represent each of the three different purposes for writing.

Answer Key
Persuade: "My passion is ecology …"; "Schools should do a better job …" Inform: "I've read everything …"; I'm an expert on astronomy …" Entertain: "After visiting the shore …"; "I have a great idea for a story …"

Author's Purpose

My passion is ecology. I think I'll write a speech about why our city should expand its recycling services.

After visiting the shore, I feel like writing a poem to describe the evening sunset.

I've read everything that's ever been written about Rosa Parks. I think I'll use that knowledge to write a biography about her.

I'm an expert on astronomy. I'd like to share that knowledge and write a book about constellations.

Schools should do a better job of preparing students for college. I want to write an editorial telling my views about how schools should improve.

I have a great idea for a story about a girl who auditions and gets a role in a Broadway play.

persuade	entertain	inform
persuade	entertain	inform

Making Inferences

Introduction

Remind students that an inference is information or a detail not directly stated in a text. Readers can use what they read, along with what they already know, to make an inference. Write this sentence on the board: *The boy picked up his umbrella and backpack and opened the door. He looked up at the sky and then put his umbrella back inside the house.* Have partners make inferences to answer the questions: *Why did the boy look up at the sky? Where is the boy going?* Have students share their ideas with the class to see if others made the same inferences.

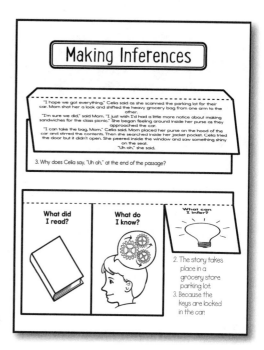

Creating the Notebook Page

Guide students through the following steps to complete the right-hand page in their notebooks.

1. Add a Table of Contents entry for the Making Inferences pages.

2. Cut out the title and glue it to the top of the page.

3. Cut out the passage flap. Apply glue to the back of the top section and attach it below the title.

4. Cut out the questions piece and glue it under the passage flap.

5. Cut out the *What did I read? What do I know? What can I infer?* flap book. Cut on the solid lines to create three flaps. Apply glue to the back of the top section and attach it below the passage flap.

6. Read the passage and discuss the event it describes. Then, read question 1 under the passage flap. Write notes for question 1 under the flap for *What did I read?* Then, write notes under the flap for *What do I know?* Finally, write your answer to question 1 under the *What can I infer?* flap.

7. Repeat step 6 for the remaining questions.

Reflect on Learning

To complete the left-hand page, have students write a paragraph that continues the story. Allow time for students to share their work.

Making Inferences

"I hope we got everything," Celia said as she scanned the parking lot for their car. Mom shot her a look and shifted the heavy grocery bag from one arm to the other.

"I'm sure we did," said Mom. "I just wish I'd had a little more notice about making sandwiches for the class picnic." She began feeling around inside her purse as they approached the car.

"I can take the bag, Mom," Celia said. Mom placed her purse on the hood of the car and stirred the contents. Then, she searched inside her jacket pocket. Celia tried the door but it didn't open. She peered inside the window and saw something shiny on the seat.

"Uh oh," she said.

1. What can you infer about Mom?

2. What can you infer about the setting?

3. Why does Celia say, "Uh oh," at the end of the passage?

What did I read?

What do I know?

What can I infer?

Comparing and Contrasting Genres

Place students in small groups and assign each group a theme or topic such as *loyalty, overcoming adversity, friendship, responsibility,* etc. Have students discuss how texts can have a similar theme even though they are from different genres. Ask groups to choose two different genres such as historical fiction and drama, or poetry and science fiction. Then, have students discuss similarities and differences in the way the topic would be covered by each.

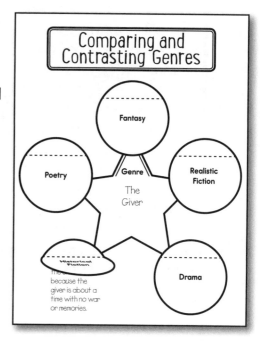

Creating the Notebook Page

Guide students through the following steps to complete the right-hand page in their notebooks.

1. Add a Table of Contents entry for the Comparing and Contrasting Genres pages.

2. Cut out the title and glue it to the top of the page.

3. Cut out the star and glue it to the center of the page.

4. Think of a recently read piece of literature and write its title on the star.

5. Cut out the genre circle flaps. Choose the genre circle flap that matches the piece of literature you wrote on the star. Apply glue to the back of the top section and attach it to the top point of the star labeled *Genre.*

6. Apply glue to the back of the top sections of the remaining genre circle flaps. Attach each one to the remaining points of the star.

7. Discuss how the piece of literature you wrote on the star might be similar or different if written in another genre. Write notes under each flap to compare and contrast it with the original genre.

Reflect on Learning

To complete the left-hand page, have students write in the voice of the author of their chosen piece of literature, explaining why he or she chose to write in that genre.

Comparing and Contrasting Genres

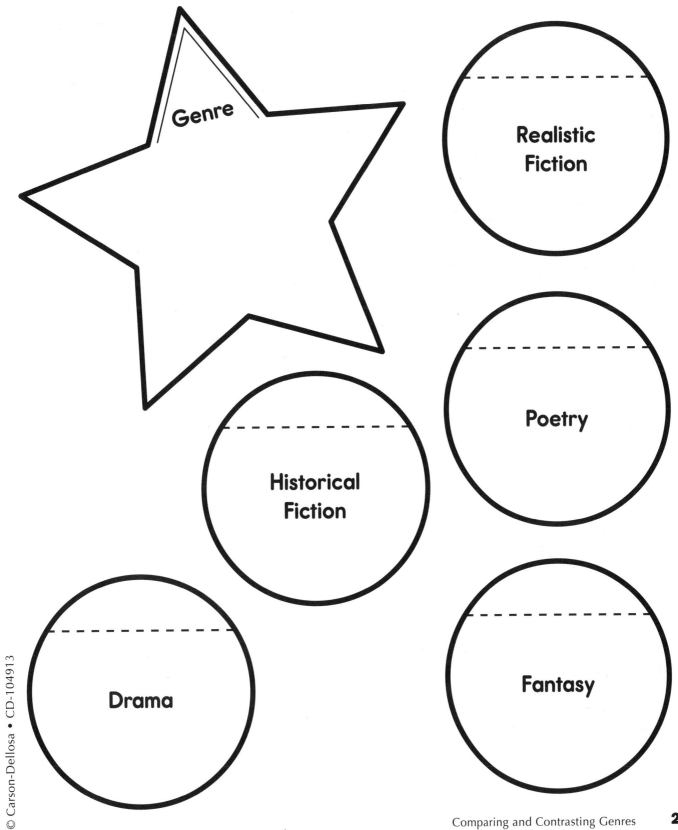

Genre

Realistic Fiction

Poetry

Historical Fiction

Drama

Fantasy

Main Idea and Summarizing

Introduction

Review the meaning of main idea and supporting details. Have students work in small groups. Assign each group a copy of a short informational text that can be cut apart. Each group should read the text and then cut the main idea and supporting details away from the rest of the text. Have students discuss the sections of text that were not part of the main idea or supporting details. Point out that the main idea and details comprise most of the text. Good writers know that unnecessary details detract from informational text and can confuse readers.

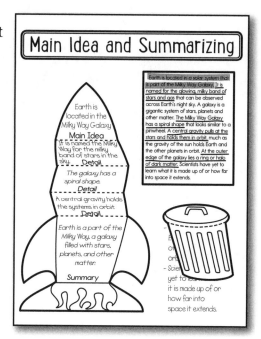

Creating the Notebook Page

Guide students through the following steps to complete the right-hand page in their notebooks.

1. Add a Table of Contents entry for the Main Idea and Summarizing pages.

2. Cut out the title and glue it to the top of the page.

3. Cut out the rocket accordion piece. Fold on the dashed lines, alternating the fold direction. Apply glue to the back of the top section and attach it to the left side of the page below the title.

4. Cut out the passage piece and glue it to the right side of the page below the title.

5. Read the passage. Highlight the main idea. Underline the details that support the main idea. Write the main idea on the top section of the rocket. Write supporting details on the three middle sections of the rocket. Write a summary of the passage on the bottom section of the rocket.

6. Cut out the trash can flap. Apply glue to the back of the top section and attach it to the bottom right of the page.

7. Look back at the passage. Find details that were not used to write the main idea or summary. Write the unused details under the flap.

Reflect on Learning

To complete the left-hand page, provide students with a copy of a short informational text to glue in their notebooks. Have them take notes on the main idea and details. Ask them to use their notes to write a summary of the text. Have partners compare their summaries.

Main Idea and Summarizing

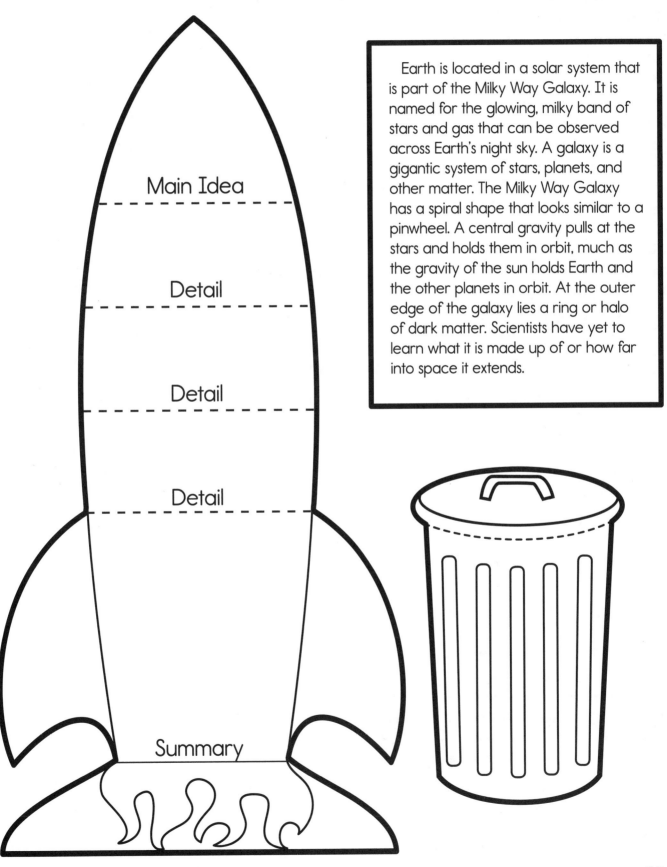

Main Idea

Detail

Detail

Detail

Summary

Earth is located in a solar system that is part of the Milky Way Galaxy. It is named for the glowing, milky band of stars and gas that can be observed across Earth's night sky. A galaxy is a gigantic system of stars, planets, and other matter. The Milky Way Galaxy has a spiral shape that looks similar to a pinwheel. A central gravity pulls at the stars and holds them in orbit, much as the gravity of the sun holds Earth and the other planets in orbit. At the outer edge of the galaxy lies a ring or halo of dark matter. Scientists have yet to learn what it is made up of or how far into space it extends.

Point of View

Introduction

Remind students that in nonfiction, point of view is an author's viewpoint or perspective on a topic. Readers can use strategies or prompts to help them determine how an author feels about a topic. For example, word choice can provide clues to an author's perspective. Provide small groups with three or four nonfiction passages representing several different points of view on the same subject. Have students read the passages and discuss how they are able to determine the point of view of each one.

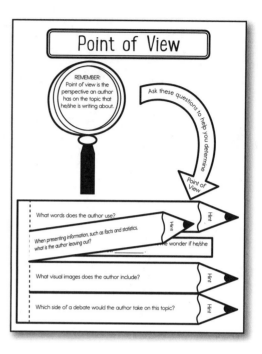

Creating the Notebook Page

Guide students through the following steps to complete the right-hand page in their notebooks.

1. Add a Table of Contents entry for the Point of View pages.

2. Cut out the title and glue it to the top of the page.

3. Cut out the magnifying glass piece and glue it to the left side of the page below the title.

4. Cut out the pencils flap book. Cut on the solid lines to create four flaps. Apply glue to the back of the left section and attach it to the bottom of the page.

5. Cut out the arrow piece and glue it to the page so that it points from the magnifying glass to the questions.

6. Cut out the sentence prompt pieces.

7. Read and discuss each prompt. Determine which question each prompt matches. Glue the prompts under the corresponding flap.

8. Use the questions and their corresponding prompts when reading an informational text to determine the author's point of view.

Reflect on Learning

To complete the left-hand page, have students choose a topic they are familiar with or have a strong feeling about and write a short paragraph on that topic. Students should highlight or underline details they include to indicate their point of view or perspective.

Point of View

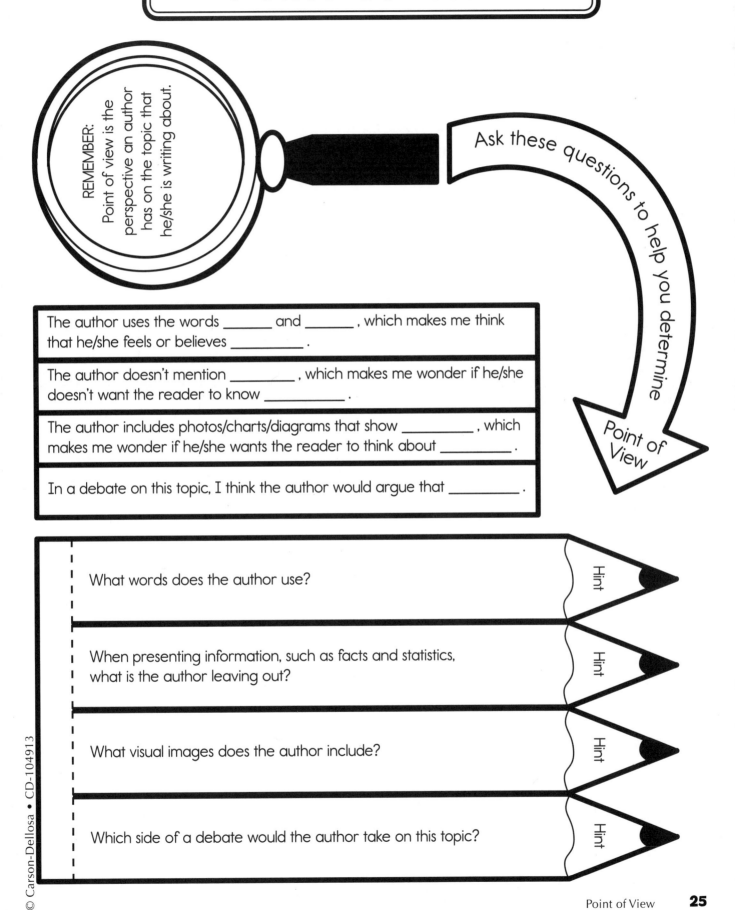

REMEMBER: Point of view is the perspective an author has on the topic that he/she is writing about.

Ask these questions to help you determine Point of View

The author uses the words _____ and _____ , which makes me think that he/she feels or believes _____ .

The author doesn't mention _____ , which makes me wonder if he/she doesn't want the reader to know _____ .

The author includes photos/charts/diagrams that show _____ , which makes me wonder if he/she wants the reader to think about _____ .

In a debate on this topic, I think the author would argue that _____ .

What words does the author use? — Hint

When presenting information, such as facts and statistics, what is the author leaving out? — Hint

What visual images does the author include? — Hint

Which side of a debate would the author take on this topic? — Hint

Text Structures

Introduction

Have small groups of students discuss the following titles and what they feel is the likely organizational structure for each one: *A Book or A Movie: Which Is Better?, What Caused the Flood of 1893?, How to Start a Pet-Sitting Business, Littering and What You Can Do About It!, The Fall Foliage Tour,* and *A Time Line of Our Town.* Have students discuss why one organizational structure may be better than another for each title.

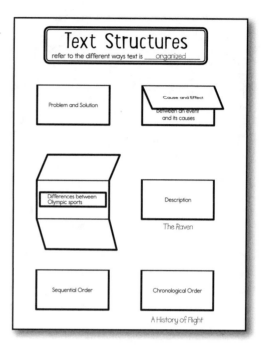

Creating the Notebook Page

Guide students through the following steps to complete the right-hand page in their notebooks.

1. Add a Table of Contents entry for the Text Structures pages.

2. Cut out the title and glue it to the top of the page.

3. Complete the explanation of *text structures* (refer to the different ways that text is **organized**).

4. Cut out the flap books. Fold on the dashed lines so that the gray glue sections are on the back of the flap books. Apply glue to the gray glue sections and attach them in a 3 by 2 grid below the title.

5. Cut out the informational text topics. Discuss the different ways that informational text can be organized. Match each topic to the best organizational structure for that topic and glue it inside the correct flap.

6. As you are read various texts, return to the page and add titles below the appropriate flap books.

Reflect on Learning

To complete the left-hand page, have students brainstorm other topics for each of the informational text structures. Ask them to write a sentence for each topic and text structure explaining why that would be the best way to organize the information.

Answer Key
Chronological Order: Important events in Lincoln's presidency; Sequential Order: How to build a bird feeder; Problem and Solution: Ways to stop beach erosion; Compare and Contrast: Differences between Olympic sports; Description: The paintings of Van Gogh; Cause and Effect: Reasons oil spills happen

Text Structures

refer to the different ways text is _____

| Important events in Lincoln's presidency | Ways to stop beach erosion | The paintings of Van Gogh |
| How to build a bird feeder | Differences between Olympic sports | Reasons why oil spills happen |

Description	glue	helps readers visualize information through descriptive sensory details	Problem and Solution	glue	introduces a problem and offers one or more solutions
Sequential Order	glue	organizes information in a sequence of steps or directions	Compare and Contrast	glue	uses comparisons to describe similarities and differences
Chronological Order	glue	presents events in a time order from beginning to end	Cause and Effect	glue	describes a relationship between an event and its causes

Planning Writing

Introduction

Remind students that writing serves three main purposes: to inform, to entertain, or to persuade. Point out that one of the first decisions a writer must make is what his or her purpose is for writing a piece. Have students name an example that they have read recently for each category of writing. Then, have students work in small groups and list different types of writing for each category. Have students share their lists with their classmates.

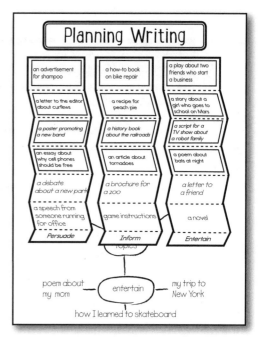

Creating the Notebook Page

Guide students through the following steps to complete the right-hand page in their notebooks.

1. Add a Table of Contents entry for the Planning Writing pages.

2. Cut out the title and glue it to the top of the page.

3. Cut out the three *Persuade, Inform,* and *Entertain* accordion pieces. Fold each piece on the dashed lines, alternating the fold direction. Apply glue to the back of the top section on each accordion piece and attach them in a row below the title.

4. Cut out the 12 writing ideas. Sort the writing ideas according to the purpose of writing that each one represents. Glue the writing ideas on the folds of the correct accordion piece.

5. On the remaining two blank folds on each accordion piece, write ideas for other types of writing for each purpose.

6. On the bottom of the page, create a bubble map with ideas for topics you could write about for each purpose.

Reflect on Learning

To complete the left-hand page, have students reflect on their favorite purpose for writing. Have them write a paragraph comparing a kind of writing they enjoy reading with what they most enjoy writing themselves.

Answer Key
Persuade: a poster promoting a new band; a letter to the editor about curfews; an essay about why cell phones should be free; an advertisement for shampoo; Inform: an article about tornadoes; a how-to book on bike repair; a recipe for peach pie; a history book about the railroads; Entertain: a story about a girl who goes to school on Mars; a poem about bats at night; a play about two friends who start a business; a script for a TV show about a robot family

28

© Carson-Dellosa • CD-104913

Planning Writing

a story about a girl who goes to school on Mars	a how-to book on bike repair	a play about two friends who start a business	an advertisement for shampoo
a poster promoting a new band	a letter to the editor about curfews	a recipe for peach pie	a script for a TV show about a robot family
an article about tornadoes	a poem about bats at night	an essay about why cell phones should be free	a history book about the railroads

Entertain						
Inform						
Persuade						

Writing an Effective Lead

Introduction

Lead a discussion with the question, "When you begin reading, how do you know if you want to continue?" Tell students that writing an effective lead, or topic sentence, is important in hooking the attention of your reader so that he or she will keep reading. Point out that a topic sentence is sometimes referred to as a *lead*, because it *leads* readers to continue reading. Provide students with self-stick notes. Have them choose lead sentences from classroom reading materials and write them on their self-stick notes. Allow students to share their leads. Then, as a group, sort the leads on the board. Do any of the leads begin with a quote, a question, an interesting fact, or a strong feeling?

Creating the Notebook Page

Guide students through the following steps to complete the right-hand page in their notebooks.

1. Add a Table of Contents entry for the Writing an Effective Lead pages.

2. Cut out the title and glue it to the top of the page.

3. Cut out the pockets. Fold over the front of each pocket. Then, apply glue to the back of the tabs and fold them around the back of each pocket. Apply glue to the back of each pocket and attach them to the page.

4. Cut out the lead sentences.

5. Read each sentence and decide what type of lead it represents. Place each lead sentence in the correct pocket.

Reflect on Learning

To complete the left-hand page, have students write two additional example sentences for each type of lead shown on the right-hand page.

Writing an Effective Lead

What would you say to someone who texts while driving?	"Space junk is a huge problem," Dr. Inez claims.
A honeybee can fly about 15 miles per hour.	Giraffes spend an average of 18 hours a day eating.
With my heart pounding, I rounded third base and headed home.	I feel that every shelter dog deserves a good home.
Should art be offered in every public school?	"I hope never to see a blizzard of that intensity again," Mrs. Liu said.

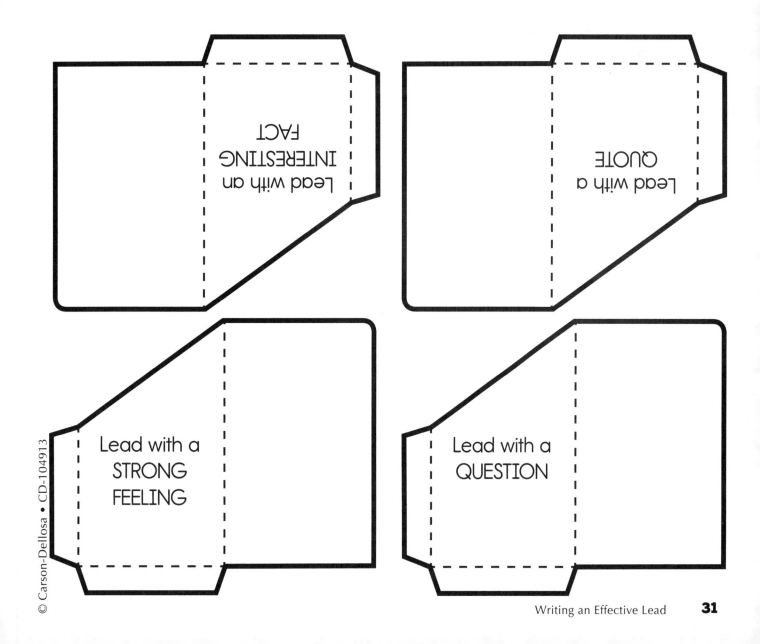

Lead with an INTERESTING FACT

Lead with a QUOTE

Lead with a STRONG FEELING

Lead with a QUESTION

Show, Don't Tell

Introduction

Remind students that an interesting personal narrative creates pictures in the minds of readers by using description that shows, rather than words that tell. Prepare five index cards with one of the following sentences on each card: *It was an unusual cat. The cat's eyes glowed yellow. Its ebony fur stood on end. The cat's pointed ears looked razor sharp. The cat let out an unearthly yowl.* Give one card to each of the five groups. Have groups discuss their card. Then, each group should read their card aloud to discover which group has a card that tells and which has a card that shows. Have students discuss the difference between *showing* and *telling* when writing descriptions.

Show, Don't Tell

means that a writer creates ___mental___ ___pictures___ for the reader. The writer uses ___description___ that ___illustrates___ people, places, and things and doesn't just ___tell___ about them.

Shiny tears rolled down the baby's chubby cheeks. Its face was flushed and hot to the touch. Silence momentarily reigned as it drew in a shaky breath.

The baby cried.

Don't just tell it! / Show it!

Jack was happy.

Don't just tell it! / Show it!

The wind blew.

Creating the Notebook Page

Guide students through the following steps to complete the right-hand page in their notebooks.

1. Add a Table of Contents entry for the Show, Don't Tell pages.

2. Cut out the title and glue it to the top of the page.

3. Complete the explanation of *show, don't tell* (means that a writer creates **mental pictures** for the reader. The writer uses **description** that **illustrates** people, places, and things and doesn't just **tell** about them).

4. Cut out the three large rectangular pieces. Fold each piece inward on the three dashed lines. Apply glue to the gray glue sections and attach the triangles to the page.

5. Cut out the three sentence pieces.

6. Read and discuss the telling sentence on each triangle. Glue the sentence piece that *shows* rather than *tells* under the flaps of the correct *Show it! Don't just tell it!* piece.

7. Write two more sentences under each flap to continue to show what is happening.

Reflect on Learning

To complete the left-hand page, have students write a paragraph that explains why writing sentences that show rather than tell about people, places, and things can improve their writing.

Show, Don't Tell

means that a writer creates _____ _____ for the reader. The writer uses _____ that _____ people, places, and things and doesn't just _____ about them.

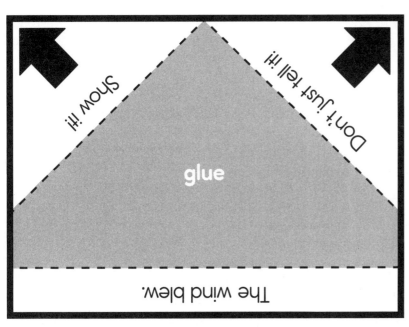

Don't just tell it!

Show it!

The wind blew.

glue

Shiny tears rolled down the baby's chubby cheeks.

The trees bent as if scared of the howling wind.

Jack couldn't hide the smile on his face that stretched from ear to ear.

Don't just tell it!

Jack was happy.

glue

Show it!

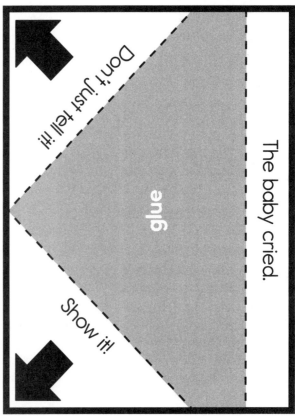

Don't just tell it!

The baby cried.

glue

Show it!

Using Sources

Introduction

Tell students about a personal hobby or interest such as gardening, history, or tennis. Then, display nonfiction books, newspapers, or magazine articles about the same topic. Remind students that a part of research writing is using sources of information. Discuss the difference between primary and secondary sources. Have students tell whether an interview with you about your hobby is a primary or secondary source (primary). Point out that primary sources are original sources and that secondary sources, like nonfiction books, etc., contain information that someone else gathered.

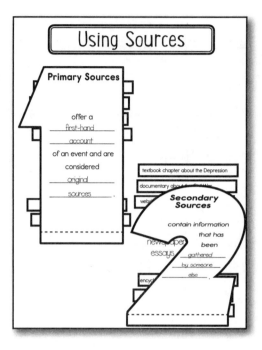

Creating the Notebook Page

Guide students through the following steps to complete the right-hand page in their notebooks.

1. Add a Table of Contents entry for the Using Sources pages.

2. Cut out the title and glue it to the top of the page.

3. Cut out the *Primary Sources* and *Secondary Sources* flaps. Apply glue to the back of the bottom sections and attach the *Primary Sources* flap to the left side of the page below the title and the *Secondary Sources* flap to the right near the bottom of the page.

4. Complete the explanations. (Primary Sources offer a **first-hand account** of an event and are considered **original sources**. Secondary Sources contain information that has been **gathered by someone else**.)

5. Cut out the sources labels. Discuss each source and determine if it is a primary or secondary source. Glue each source under the correct flap. Add your own ideas for primary and secondary sources and write them under the flaps.

Reflect on Learning

To complete the left-hand page, have students write a paragraph that explains why they should evaluate both primary and secondary sources before using them in their research.

Answer Key
Primary sources: interview with the mayor; original map of a city subway system; tool used to build an early railroad; diary written by Martha Washington; poster from Kennedy's presidential campaign; recording of an early jazz musician. Secondary sources: documentary about the Civil War; encyclopedia entry on NASA; TV show about extreme weather; website review of a book; magazine article on beekeeping; textbook chapter about the Depression

Using Sources

interview with the mayor	TV show about extreme weather
documentary about the Civil War	textbook chapter about the Depression
encyclopedia entry on NASA	tool used to build an early railroad
original map of a city subway system	website review of a book

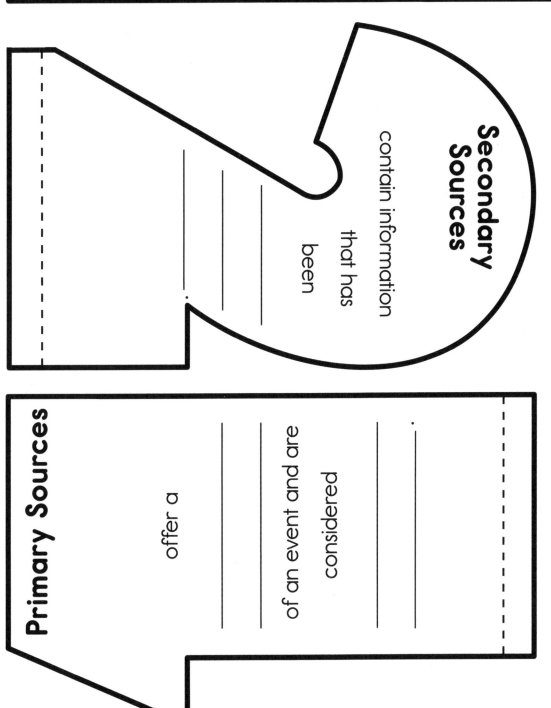

Secondary Sources

contain information

that has

been

Primary Sources

offer a

of an event and are

considered

diary written by Martha Washington

poster from Kennedy's presidential campaign

recording of an early jazz musician

magazine article on beekeeping

Proofreading

Introduction

Before class, prepare eight index cards with each card showing one of eight proofreading marks. Include marks for the following: *add a letter, word, or words; add a period; add a comma; delete a letter, word, or words; make a capital letter; make a lowercase letter; reverse letters or words;* and *begin a new paragraph.* Discuss how and when each mark is used. Then, write a paragraph on the board that contains one each type of mistake. Have students use the cards to correct the paragraph on the board. Finally, have them rewrite the corrected piece.

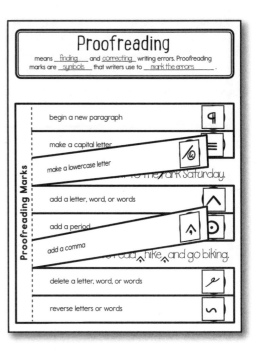

Creating the Notebook Page

Guide students through the following steps to complete the right-hand page in their notebooks.

1. Add a Table of Contents entry for the Proofreading pages.

2. Cut out the title and glue it to the top of the page.

3. Complete the explanation of *proofreading* (means **finding** and **correcting** writing errors. Proofreading marks are **symbols** that writers use to **mark the errors**).

4. Cut out the *Proofreading Marks* flap book. Cut on the solid lines to create eight flaps. Apply glue to the back of the left section and attach it to the page.

5. Cut out the eight proofreading symbol pieces. Glue each proofreading mark to the circle on the correct flap.

6. Under each flap, write an example that shows the proofreading mark being used to correct an error. Use this page as a guide the next time you need to proofread your writing.

Reflect on Learning

To complete the left-hand page, have students write a quick letter to a friend or family member. Then, ask them to exchange letters with a partner and use proofreading marks to correct any errors.

Answer Key
¶ begin a new paragraph; ≡ make a capital letter; ⧸⊘ make a lowercase letter; ∧ add a letter, word, or words; ⊙ add a period; ⋏ add a comma; ⅊ delete a letter, word, or words; ∾ reverse letters or words

Proofreading

means _____ and _____ writing errors. Proofreading
marks are _____ that writers use to _____ .

⊙	/lc	∧	¶	☰	∿	ℓ	⌃

Proofreading Marks

begin a new paragraph	◯
make a capital letter	◯
make a lowercase letter	◯
add a letter, word, or words	◯
add a period	◯
add a comma	◯
delete a letter, word, or words	◯
reverse letters or words	◯

Parts of Speech

Introduction

Before the lesson, prepare eight index cards with the following parts of speech: *noun, pronoun, verb, preposition, adjective, adverb, conjunction,* and *interjection.* Divide the class into eight groups and give each group a card. Tell students that each word in a sentence has a job. Ask students to write the job description for the part of speech on their cards. Then, read several sentences slowly and have students hold up their cards to identify the part of speech for each word in the sentence.

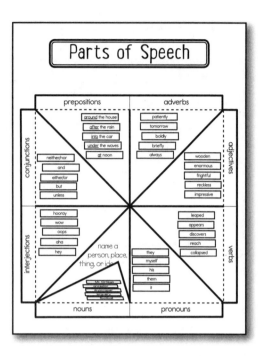

Creating the Notebook Page

Guide students through the following steps to complete the right-hand page in their notebooks.

1. Add a Table of Contents entry for the Parts of Speech pages.

2. Cut out the title and glue it to the top of the page.

3. Cut out the parts of speech flaps. Cut each flap on the solid line to create two flaps. Apply glue to the back of the text section of each flap. Attach the flaps in the center of the page so that all of the points touch in the center.

4. Cut out the word pieces. Glue each word onto the flap that matches the word's part of speech.

5. Under each flap, write the purpose of that part of speech.

Reflect on Learning

To complete the left-hand page, have students write a short essay about something that they are afraid of. Have students create a color key for each part of speech. Then have them use the colors to highlight each word in the essay to identify its part of speech. For example, nouns are blue, verbs are red, etc.

Answer Key
Nouns: Mr. Ortega, skyscraper, ancestor, bravery, football; name a person, place, thing, or idea; Pronouns: they, it, his, them, myself; are used in place of a noun; Verbs: leaped, appears, reach, collapsed, discovers; shows action or links a subject to another word in the sentence; Adjectives: enormous, impressive, frightful, reckless, wooden; describe a noun or pronoun; Adverbs: always, boldly, briefly, tomorrow, patiently; describe a verb, adjective, or another adverb; Prepositions: into the car, under the waves, around the house, after the rain, at noon; show position or direction and introduces prepositional phrases; Conjunctions: and, but, either/or, neither/nor, unless; connect other words or groups of words; Interjections: wow, aha, oops, hey, hooray; show strong emotion.

Parts of Speech

<u>after</u> the rain	boldly	football	leaped	skyscraper
aha	bravery	frightful	Mr. Ortega	them
always	briefly	hey	myself	they
ancestor	but	his	neither/nor	tomorrow
and	collapsed	hooray	oops	<u>under</u> the waves
appears	discovers	impressive	patiently	unless
<u>around</u> the house	either/or	<u>into</u> the car	reach	wooden
<u>at</u> noon	enormous	it	reckless	wow

prepositions

adverbs

conjunctions

adjectives

interjections

verbs

nouns

pronouns

Types of Nouns

Introduction

Review that a noun names a person, place, thing, or idea. Write the following nouns on the board: *Statue of Liberty*, *river*, *box*, *courage*, and *audience*. Point out that each word represents a different type of noun. Have students work in small groups to match each noun with its corresponding type: *proper noun*, *common noun*, *concrete noun*, *abstract noun*, and *collective noun*. Discuss how some nouns may belong to more than one category. Then, have groups list other examples for each type. Have students share their lists.

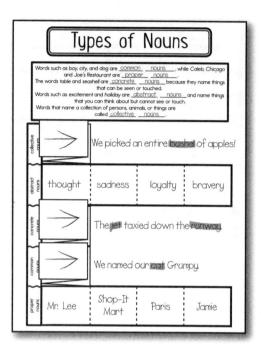

Creating the Notebook Page

Guide students through the following steps to complete the right-hand page in their notebooks.

1. Add a Table of Contents entry for the Types of Nouns pages.

2. Cut out the title and glue it to the top of the page.

3. Cut out the *Words such as* piece and glue it below the title.

4. Complete the sentences. (Words such as *boy*, *city*, and *dog* are **common nouns**, while *Caleb*, *Chicago*, and *Joe's Restaurant* are **proper nouns**. The words *table* and *seashell* are **concrete nouns** because they name things that can be seen or touched. Words such as *excitement* and *holiday* are **abstract nouns** and name things that you can think about but cannot see or touch. Words that name a collection of persons, animals, or things are called **collective nouns**.)

5. Cut out the types of nouns accordion flap book. Cut on the solid lines to create five flaps. Fold each section on the dashed lines, alternating the fold direction. Apply glue to the back of the left section of the flap book and attach it to the page.

6. On each of the accordion folds, write nouns that are examples of each type listed. Next to each folded accordion book, write a sentence containing at least one example of that noun type. Highlight or underline the noun or nouns used.

Reflect on Learning

To complete the left-hand page, give students access to newspapers, magazine articles, or other reading materials. Have them find and list five examples of each type of noun.

Types of Nouns

Words such as *boy, city,* and *dog* are _____ _____ , while *Caleb, Chicago,* and *Joe's Restaurant* are _____ _____ .

The words *table* and *seashell* are _____ _____ because they name things that can be seen or touched.

Words such as *excitement* and *holiday* are _____ _____ and name things that you can think about but cannot see or touch.

Words that name a collection of persons, animals, or things are called _____ _____ .

collective nouns			
abstract nouns			
concrete nouns			
common nouns			
proper nouns			

Using Pronouns

Review pronouns and antecedents. Write this sentence on the board: *As Krista walked into Krista's classroom, Krista first thought that Krista had forgotten Krista's lunch until Krista saw Krista's lunch in Krista's backpack.* Have students discuss why the sentence sounds awkward and confusing. Tell students that pronouns can be used to help writing flow more smoothly. Have partners rewrite the sentence using pronouns. Allow time for students to share their sentences.

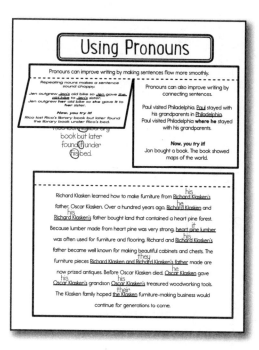

Creating the Notebook Page

Guide students through the following steps to complete the right-hand page in their notebooks.

1. Add a Table of Contents entry for the Using Pronouns pages.

2. Cut out the title and glue it to the top of the page.

3. Cut out the *Pronouns can improve writing* flap book. Cut on the solid line to create two flaps. Apply glue to the back of the top section and glue it below the title.

4. Discuss how pronouns are used in both examples to make the writing flow more smoothly. Write a sentence under each flap to improve the *Now, you try it!* sentences. Circle the pronouns.

5. Cut out the text passage flap. Apply glue to the back of the top section and attach it to the bottom of the page.

6. Read the passage. Above each underlined noun, write a pronoun to replace it.

7. Rewrite the improved passage under the flap.

Reflect on Learning

To complete the left-hand page, have students imagine that they are speaking with someone who is unfamiliar with using pronouns. Students should write a paragraph that explains how writing can be improved by using pronouns to correct choppy sentences and to combine sentences.

Using Verb Tenses

Simple Present	Present Perfect	Present Progressive
Simple Present I paint every day.	**Present Perfect** I have painted today.	**Present Progressive** I am painting right now.
Simple Past I painted yesterday.	**Past Perfect** I had painted yesterday.	**Past Progressive** I was painting last week.
Simple Future I will paint tomorrow.	**Future Perfect** I will have painted every day by next week.	**Future Progressive** I will be painting again next week.

Simple Present: I help Mom every day.

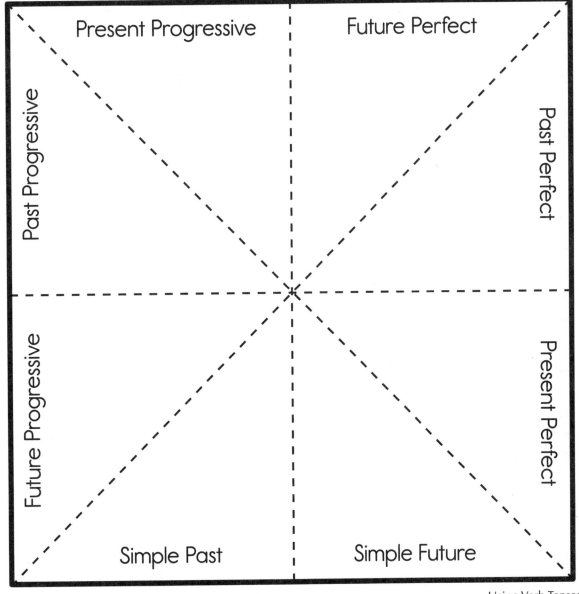

Active and Passive Voice

Remind students that if a verb is in the active voice, the subject is doing the action. If a verb is in the passive voice, the subject is being acted upon. Read aloud several example sentences. If the sentence is written in the active voice, have students stand up and shake their arms above their heads. If the sentence is passive, have them sit very still. Use these sentences to begin: *The essay was written quickly by the frantic student.* (passive) *The student frantically wrote the essay.* (active) Continue with other active and passive examples. Have students discuss which sentences sound stronger and why.

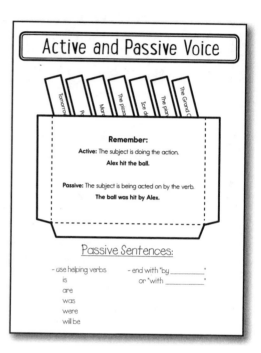

Creating the Notebook Page

Guide students through the following steps to complete the right-hand page in their notebooks.

1. Add a Table of Contents entry for the Active and Passive Voice pages.

2. Cut out the title and glue it to the top of the page.

3. Cut out the pocket. Apply glue to the back of the tabs and attach the pocket to the center of the page.

4. Cut out the sentences. Sort the sentences into two groups: active voice and passive voice. Match each active voice sentence with its passive voice counterpart by gluing them back-to-back.

5. Write a checkmark next to the active voice sentence. Write an **X** next to the passive voice sentence. Place the sentences in the pocket.

6. Review all of the passive voice sentences and look for similarities. List the characteristics of passive voice sentences at the bottom of the page.

Reflect on Learning

To complete the left-hand page, have students review a recent piece of their writing. Students should identify and record at least one example of a passive sentence. Then, have students rewrite the sentence in the active voice and describe how it makes the writing stronger.

© Carson-Dellosa • CD-104913

Active and Passive Voice

The Grand Canyon is visited by many tourists.	Congress passed a new bill.
The piano solo was played by Marco.	The orange trees were destroyed by ice.
Ice destroyed the orange trees.	Mrs. Lee baked three dozen cookies for the bake sale.
The pizzas were eaten by the students.	A new bill was passed by Congress.
Marco played the piano solo.	Most students prefer a longer recess.
Anita and Dave will clean the kitchen.	Many tourists visit the Grand Canyon.
Popcorn filled the bowl.	For the bake sale, three dozen cookies were baked by Mrs. Lee.
Tomorrow the team will celebrate the championship.	The movie review was written by Terence.
The bowl was filled with popcorn.	The kitchen will be cleaned by Anita and Dave.
Terence wrote a movie review.	The championship will be celebrated by the team tomorrow.
The students ate the pizzas.	A longer recess is preferred by most students.

Remember:

Active: The subject is doing the action.

Alex hit the ball.

Passive: The subject is being acted on by the verb.

The ball was hit by Alex.

Using Adjectives to Compare

Introduction

Remind students that an adjective is used to describe a noun or pronoun. When making comparisons, adjectives change form according to the number of items being compared. Identify two objects in the classroom that can be compared. For example, two books of different sizes. Have students write a sentence using the comparative form of *big* to describe the books. Add a third book. Have students write a sentence using the superlative form. Have students work in groups and continue the activity with other objects in the classroom.

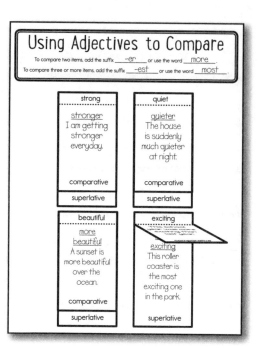

Creating the Notebook Page

Guide students through the following steps to complete the right-hand page in their notebooks.

1. Add a Table of Contents entry for the Using Adjectives to Compare pages.

2. Cut out the title and glue it to the top of the page.

3. Complete the explanation. (To compare two items, add the suffix **–er** or use the word **more**. To compare three or more items, add the suffix **–est** or use the word **most**.)

4. Cut out the *comparative* and *superlative* flaps. Apply glue to the gray glue section of each *superlative* flap. Place a comparative flap on top to create a stacked two-flap book. Repeat for all flaps. Make sure that the word *superlative* is visible below each layered tab. Glue the flaps in a 2 by 2 grid on the page.

5. Read each adjective. Write the comparative form for each on the *comparative* flap, along with a sentence using the comparative form. Write the superlative form for each on the *superlative* flap, along with a sentence using the superlative form.

Reflect on Learning

To complete the left-hand page, have students make a list of four additional adjectives and then write the comparative and superlative forms of each. Students should write a sentence using each word.

Using Adjectives to Compare

To compare two items, add the suffix _____ or use the word _____.

To compare three or more items, add the suffix _____ or use the word _____.

exciting	comparative	glue	superlative
quiet	comparative	glue	superlative
beautiful	comparative	glue	superlative
strong	comparative	glue	superlative

© Carson-Dellosa • CD-104913

Adverbs

Introduction

Remind students that adverbs are words and phrases that modify verbs, adjectives, and other adverbs. Ask students to take out a pencil and paper. Tell them to write a paragraph telling what they did last weekend, but they may not use any adverbs in their writing. When they have finished, ask them to exchange papers with a partner and mark through any adverbs that may have been missed. Tell them to look for words or phrases that tell when, where, how, or how often an action takes place. Have students discuss the difficulty in writing without using adverbs.

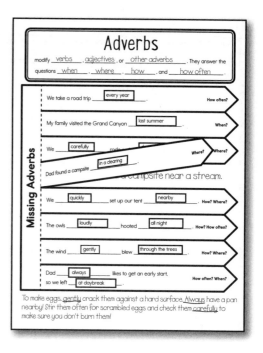

Creating the Notebook Page

Guide students through the following steps to complete the right-hand page in their notebooks.

1. Add a Table of Contents entry for the Adverbs pages.

2. Cut out the title and glue it to the top of the page.

3. Complete the definition of adverbs. (modify **verbs**, **adjectives**, or **other adverbs**. They answer the questions **when**, **where**, **how** and **how often**.)

4. Cut out the *Missing Adverbs* flap book. Cut on the solid lines to create eight flaps. Apply glue to the back of the left side and attach it to the page below the title.

5. Cut out the adverb words and phrases. Discuss which question each word or phrase answers: *when*, *where*, *how*, or *how often*. Glue each adverb or adverb phrase to the correct place in each sentence.

6. Under each flap, rewrite the sentence using a different adverb or adverbial phrase.

7. On the bottom of the page, write a sentence or two using several of the adverbs or adverbial phrases above. Underline each.

Reflect on Learning

To complete the left-hand page, have students open a book in their desk and identify 10 adverbs or adverb phrases. Students should categorize the words according to which question they answer.

Answer Key
Answers will vary but may include: We take a road trip every year. My family visited the Grand Canyon last summer. We carefully rode mules down steep trails. Dad found a campsite nearby. We quickly set up our tent in a clearing. The owls loudly hooted all night. The wind gently blew through the trees. Dad always likes to get an early start, so we left at daybreak.

Adverbs

modify _____ , _____ , or _____ . They answer
the questions _____ , _____ , _____ , and _____ .

Missing Adverbs

We take a road trip _____ . **How often?**

My family visited the Grand Canyon _____ . **When?**

We _____ rode mules _____ . **How? Where?**

Dad found a campsite _____ . **Where?**

We _____ set up our tent _____ . **How? Where?**

The owls _____ hooted _____ . **How? How often?**

The wind _____ blew _____ . **How? Where?**

Dad _____ likes to get an early start,
so we left _____ . **How often? When?**

last summer	every year	all night	always
at daybreak	carefully	quickly	
loudly	gently	in a clearing	
down steep trails	nearby	through the trees	

Using Prepositional Phrases

Introduction

Review prepositions. Write this sentence on the board: *The frog jumped into the pond.* Have students identify the prepositional phrase (into the pond). Explain that often a prepositional phrase is placed at the end of a sentence. Write this sentence on the board: *Into the pond, the frog jumped.* Point out that writers can change the placement of prepositional phrases to make their writing more interesting. Write the following prepositional phrases on the board: *above the clouds,* and *between the book's pages.* Ask partners to write two sentences for each prepositional phrase, placing the phrases in different positions.

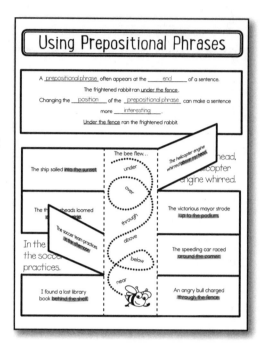

Creating the Notebook Page

Guide students through the following steps to complete the right-hand page in their notebooks.

1. Add a Table of Contents entry for the Using Prepositional Phrases pages.

2. Cut out the title and glue it to the top of the page.

3. Cut out the *A ___ often appears* piece and glue it below the title.

4. Discuss prepositional phrases and how placement can change the sentence pattern and make writing more interesting. Complete the sentences. (A **prepositional phrase** often appears at the **end** of a sentence. Changing the **position** of the **prepositional phrase** can make a sentence more **interesting**.)

5. Cut out the flap book. Cut on the solid lines to create eight flaps. Apply glue to the back of the center section and attach it to the page.

6. Read each sentence. Highlight the prepositional phrase. Rewrite the sentence under the flap, changing the position of the prepositional phrase. Make sure that the meaning of the sentence doesn't change.

Reflect on Learning

To complete the left-hand page, have students write a sentence for each of the prepositions in the center section of the flap book. Students should write a second sentence for each preposition, changing the placement of each prepositional phrase in the original sentence.

Using Prepositional Phrases

A _____ often appears at the _____ of a sentence.

The frightened rabbit ran <u>under the fence</u>.

Changing the _____ of the _____ can make a sentence more _____.

<u>Under the fence</u> ran the frightened rabbit.

The ship sailed into the sunset.

The thunderheads loomed over the prairie.

The soccer team practices in the afternoon

I found a lost library book behind the shelf.

The bee flew…

under

over

through

above

below

near

The helicopter engine whirred above my head.

The victorious mayor strode up to the podium.

The speeding car raced around the corner.

An angry bull charged through the fence.

Subordinating Conjunctions

Remind students that a conjunction joins words or groups of words in a sentence. Write the following on the board: *The boy did his homework / before he played a video game.* Explain that one clause is independent and one is dependent. The word *before* is a subordinating conjunction and is part of the dependent clause, which means it cannot stand alone as a sentence. Have students write a sentence using the clauses. Write several independent and dependent clauses on the board. Have students combine the clauses to create complete sentences.

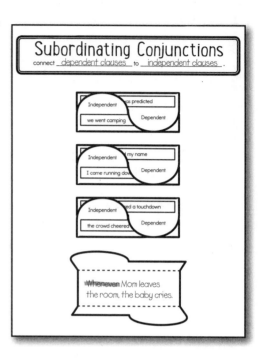

Creating the Notebook Page

Guide students through the following steps to complete the right-hand page in their notebooks.

1. Add a Table of Contents entry for the Subordinating Conjunctions pages.

2. Cut out the title and glue it to the top of the page.

3. Complete the definition of *subordinating conjunctions* (connect **dependent clauses** to **independent clauses**).

4. Cut out the interlocking booklets. With the blank sides faceup, fold the tops and bottoms in on the dashed lines. Apply glue to the gray glue sections and attach the four booklets to the page.

5. Cut out the clause pieces. Match each dependent clause to the correct independent clause to create a complete sentence. Glue the pair of clauses on top of the correct flaps of each interlocking booklet.

6. Open the booklet and write a complete sentence using the clauses. Remember that if a dependent clause begins a sentence, it is standard to add a comma to separate it from the independent clause, but if it ends a sentence, a comma is not used. Highlight the subordinating conjunction in each sentence. Make sure to add correct capitalization and punctuation.

Reflect on Learning

To complete the left-hand page, give students a variety of reading materials. Have them find and write eight sentences that contain subordinating conjunctions. Ask them to use three different colors to highlight the independent clause, dependent clause, and subordinating conjunction in each sentence.

Subordinating Conjunctions

connect _____ _____ to _____ _____ .

whenever Mom leaves the room	even though rain was predicted
just as Dad called my name	the crowd cheered loudly
we went camping	when the team scored a touchdown
the baby cries	I came running down the steps

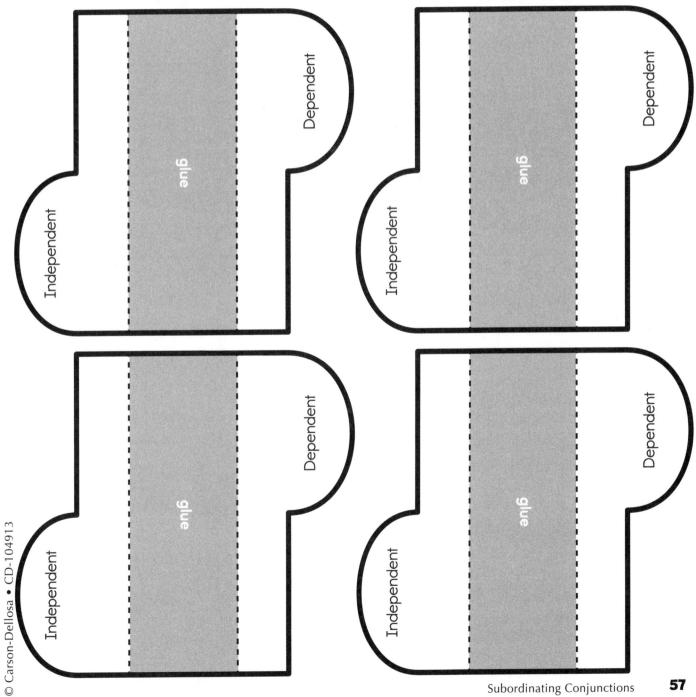

Coordinating Conjunctions

Introduction

Distribute copies of several different newspaper or magazine articles to students. Ask them to mark through any of the following conjunctions that appear in the piece: *for, and, nor, but, or, yet,* and *so.* Have partners read the articles to each other. Discuss how the missing conjunctions affect their comprehension of the piece.

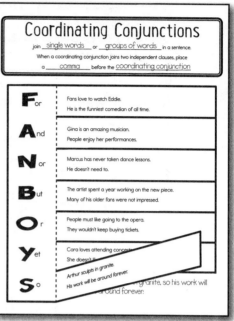

Creating the Notebook Page

Guide students through the following steps to complete the right-hand page in their notebooks.

1. Add a Table of Contents entry for the Coordinating Conjunctions pages.

2. Cut out the title and glue it to the top of the page.

3. Complete the definition for *coordinating conjunctions* (join **single words** or **groups of words** in a sentence. When a coordinating conjunction joins two independent clauses, place a **comma** before the **coordinating conjunction**).

4. Cut out the flap book. Cut on the solid lines to create seven flaps. Apply glue to the back of the left side and attach it below the title.

5. Discuss the acronym FANBOYS and how it can help you remember the coordinating conjunctions *for, and, nor, but, or, yet,* and *so.*

6. Read the pair of sentences on each flap. Combine the sentences using the coordinating conjunction for each pair. Write the new sentences under the flaps.

Reflect on Learning

To complete the left-hand page, have each student write the text for an email to a friend describing an unusual, imaginary day. Students should use as many coordinating conjunctions as possible, highlighting each one.

Coordinating Conjunctions

join _____ or _____ in a sentence.

When a coordinating conjunction joins two independent clauses, place

a _____ before the _____ .

For	Fans love to watch Eddie. He is the funniest comedian of all time.
And	Gina is an amazing musician. People enjoy her performances.
Nor	Marcus has never taken dance lessons. He doesn't need to.
But	The artist spent a year working on the new piece. Many of his older fans were not impressed.
Or	People must like going to the opera. They wouldn't keep buying tickets.
Yet	Cara loves attending concerts. She doesn't like big crowds.
So	Arthur sculpts in granite. His work will be around forever.

Appositives

Write the following two sentences on the board: *Kenan played a piano solo by Mozart. Kenan played a piano solo by Mozart, his favorite composer.* Have students discuss which sentence is more descriptive. Underline the phrase *his favorite composer.* Tell students that the phrase is an appositive. An appositive is a word or phrase that identifies a noun or gives additional information about it. Point out that appositives are set apart from the rest of the sentence with commas. Give students three simple sentences and ask them to add an appositive to each one.

Creating the Notebook Page

Guide students through the following steps to complete the right-hand page in their notebooks.

1. Add a Table of Contents entry for the Appositives pages.

2. Cut out the title and glue it to the top of the page.

3. Cut out the *An appositive is* piece and glue it below the title.

4. Discuss appositives and how they can improve the sound of choppy sentences. Read the examples. Complete the explanation. (An appositive is a **word** or **phrase** that describes or gives more information about a **noun**. Appositives can make **choppy** sentences sound **smoother**. Use **commas** to set apart an appositive from the rest of the sentence.)

5. Cut out the 14 sentence pieces. Match each appositive to the noun it describes and to the correct verb phrase. Glue the matching pieces to the page to create five sentences. Add commas to set apart each appositive from the rest of the sentence. Add periods to the end of each sentence.

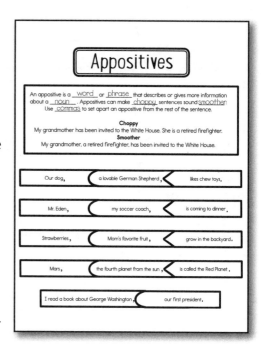

Reflect on Learning

To complete the left-hand page, have students find five sentences from books, magazine articles, newspapers, or other print materials that could be improved by adding appositives. Have students write the original sentences and the improved sentences.

Answer Key
Our dog, a lovable German shepherd, likes chew toys. Strawberries, Mom's favorite fruit, grow in the backyard. Mars, the fourth planet from the sun, is called the Red Planet. Mr. Eden, my soccer coach, is coming to dinner. I read a book about George Washington, our first president.

Appositives

An appositive is a _____ or _____ that describes or gives more information about a _____ . Appositives can make _____ sentences sound _____ . Use _____ to set apart an appositive from the rest of the sentence.

Choppy
My grandmother has been invited to the White House. She is a retired firefighter.
Smoother
My grandmother, a retired firefighter, has been invited to the White House.

Our dog

Mr. Eden

Strawberries

our first president

Mars

grow in the backyard

my soccer coach

is coming to dinner

likes chew toys

a lovable German shepherd

Mom's favorite fruit

the fourth planet from the sun

is called the Red Planet

I read a book about George Washington

Punctuating Clauses

Write the following sentences on the board: *The campers who want to canoe should go to the dock. Gemma, who enjoys canoeing, is a camp counselor.* Have students identify the clauses. (*who want to canoe*; *who enjoys canoeing*) Cover the clauses and have students read again. Explain that the first example contains a restrictive clause, meaning that the clause is essential to understanding the sentence. The second example contains a nonrestrictive clause, meaning that the clause is not essential to the meaning of the sentence. Point out that commas are used to set apart nonrestrictive clauses.

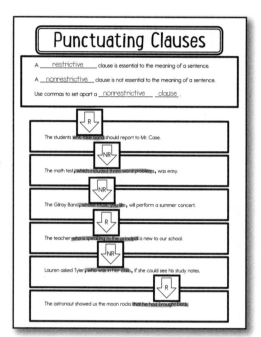

Creating the Notebook Page

Guide students through the following steps to complete the right-hand page in their notebooks.

1. Add a Table of Contents entry for the Punctuating Clauses pages.

2. Cut out the title and glue it to the top of the page.

3. Cut out the *A _____ clause* piece and glue it below the title.

4. Complete the definitions. (A **restrictive** clause is essential to the meaning of a sentence. A **nonrestrictive** clause is not essential to the meaning of a sentence. Use commas to set apart a **nonrestrictive clause**.)

5. Cut out the sentence pieces and glue them below the *A ____ clause* piece.

6. Cut out the arrow pieces.

7. Read each sentence. Highlight or underline the clause in each sentence. Glue an *R* piece above restrictive clauses. Glue an *NR* piece above the nonrestrictive clauses. Not all arrows will be used.

8. Add commas where needed to the sentences with nonrestrictive clauses.

Reflect on Learning

To complete the left-hand page, have students identify five clauses in articles, magazines, or books. Students should underline each clause and mark it as restrictive or nonrestrictive.

Answer Key
Restrictive: who take band, that he had brought back, who is speaking to the principal; Nonrestrictive: which included three word problems, whose music you like, who was in her class; Check all nonrestrictive clauses for proper comma placement.

Punctuating Clauses

A _____ clause is essential to the meaning of a sentence.

A _____ clause is not essential to the meaning of a sentence.

Use commas to set apart a _____ _____.

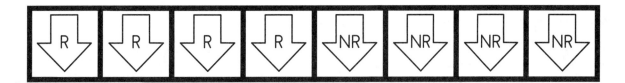

The students who take band should report to Mr. Case.

The math test which included three word problems was easy.

The Gilroy Band whose music you like will perform a summer concert.

The teacher who is speaking to the principal is new to our school.

Lauren asked Tyler who was in her class if she could see his study notes.

The astronaut showed us the moon rocks that he had brought back.

Fragments and Run-On Sentences

Introduction

Write a fragment on the board, such as *The players*, or *jumping up and down in excitement*. As a class, discuss whether the sentences were understandable and why or why not. Then, have students work with a partner to change the fragment to a complete sentence. Allow several students to share, then discuss what their changes had in common (adding a missing subject or verb). Repeat with a run-on sentence. Discuss the different ways of fixing run-on sentences.

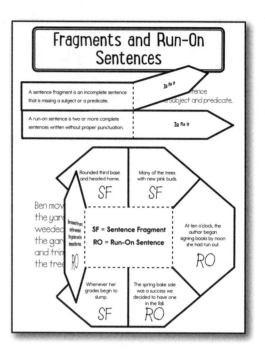

Creating the Notebook Page

Guide students through the following steps to complete the right-hand page in their notebooks.

1. Add a Table of Contents entry for the Fragments and Run-On Sentences pages.

2. Cut out the title and glue it to the top of the page.

3. Cut out the *A sentence fragment is* piece. Cut on the solid line to create two flaps. Apply glue to the back of the left side and attach the piece below the title.

4. Discuss each type of sentence. Under each flap, write one or more ways to correct a sentence fragment and run-on sentence.

5. Cut out the flap book. Cut on the solid lines to create six flaps. Apply glue to the back of the center section and attach it to the bottom of the page.

6. Read each sentence. Write SF on the flap if it is a sentence fragment and RO if it is a run-on sentence. Under the flap, write a corrected version of the sentence fragment or run-on sentence.

Reflect on Learning

To complete the left-hand page, have students create a checklist of questions that writers could ask to determine if any of their sentences are fragments or run-ons. For example: *Does my sentence contain both a subject and a predicate?*

Fragments and Run-On Sentences

A sentence fragment is an incomplete sentence that is missing a subject or a predicate.

To fix it

A run-on sentence is two or more complete sentences written without proper punctuation.

To fix it

Rounded third base and headed home.

Many of the trees with new pink buds.

Ben mowed the yard and he weeded the garden and he trimmed the trees.

SF = Sentence Fragment

RO = Run-On Sentence

At ten o'clock, the author began signing books by noon she had run out.

Whenever her grades begin to slump.

The spring bake sale was a success we decided to have one in the fall.

Shades of Meaning

Introduction

Remind students that synonyms are words with similar meanings. Point out that even though the meanings are similar, the words are not always interchangeable. Words can have different shades of meaning. Write the words *laugh* and *cackle* on the board. Ask students to demonstrate each word. Then, ask which word has a more positive connotation or feeling and which has a more negative feeling. Have partners do the same with *hurried/charged* and *reached for/grabbed*.

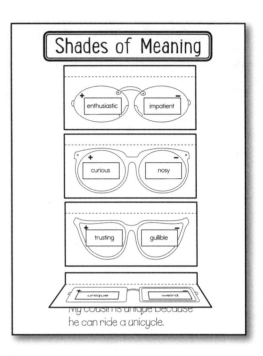

Creating the Notebook Page

Guide students through the following steps to complete the right-hand page in their notebooks.

1. Add a Table of Contents entry for the Shades of Meaning pages.

2. Cut out the title and glue it to the top of the page.

3. Cut out the sunglasses flaps. Apply glue to the back of the top section of each flap and attach them to the page.

4. Cut out the word cards.

5. Match the synonyms. Discuss how some synonyms can have a positive or negative connotation. Glue the synonym with a positive connotation to the left lens of each shade. Glue its matching synonym with a negative connotation to the right lens of the same sunglasses.

6. Under each flap, choose one of the synonyms and write a sentence. The sentence should reflect the correct connotation of each word.

Reflect on Learning

To complete the left-hand page, write the word pairs *cheap* and *thrifty* and *determined* and *stubborn* on the board. Have students place them in a T-chart showing which word in each pair has a positive connotation and which one has a negative connotation. Then, students should write a short story using all four words correctly.

Answer Key
curious/nosy; enthusiastic/impatient; trusting/gullible; unique/weird

Shades of Meaning

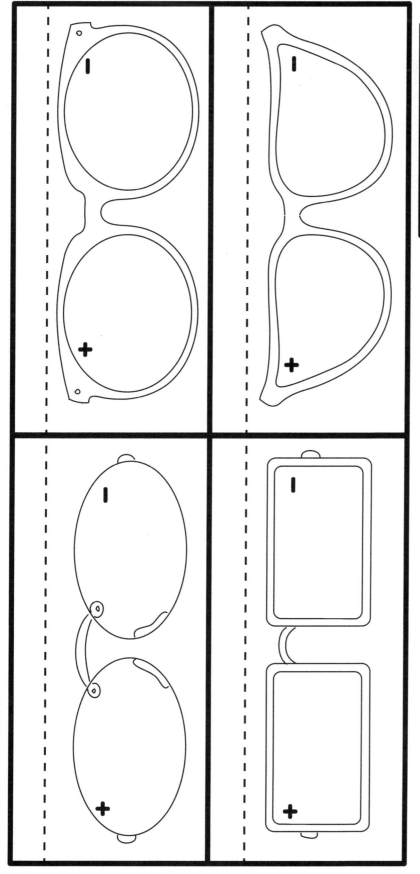

curious	nosy
enthusiastic	trusting
gullible	unique
impatient	weird

Understanding Idioms

Introduction

Review the definition of the word *idiom*. Before class, prepare a set of cards so that each student has one card. On half of the cards, write commonly used idioms. On the other half, write the meanings of the idioms. Distribute the cards and ask each student to try to find the student who has his or her matching card. Make the activity more challenging by telling students they may not show their cards or speak.

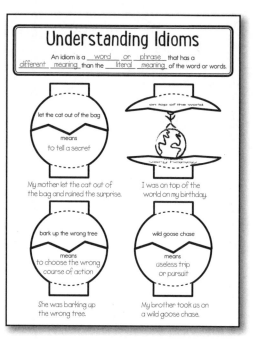

Creating the Notebook Page

Guide students through the following steps to complete the right-hand page in their notebooks.

1. Add a Table of Contents entry for the Understanding Idioms pages.

2. Cut out the title and glue it to the top of the page.

3. Complete the definition of an idiom. (An idiom is a **word or phrase** that has a **different meaning** than the **literal meaning** of the word or words.)

4. Cut out the puzzle flaps. Match the shapes to create four circles. Apply glue to the narrow strip on each of the flaps and attach the matching shapes to the page, leaving room below each one to write a sentence.

5. Discuss the idioms on each flap. On its matching flap, write the meaning for the idiom.

6. Under each pair of flaps, draw a picture showing the literal meaning of the idiom. Below each flap, write a sentence using the idiom.

Reflect on Learning

To complete the left-hand page, have students write a paragraph using as many idioms as possible. Ask them to exchange notebooks with a partner and rewrite their partner's paragraph, replacing the idioms with the actual meaning of the idioms.

Answer Key
wild goose chase/a useless trip or pursuit; on top of the world/very happy; to let the cat out of the bag/to tell a secret; bark up the wrong tree/choose the wrong course of action

Understanding Idioms

An idiom is a _____ ___ _____ that has a
_____ _____ than the _____ _____ of the word or words.

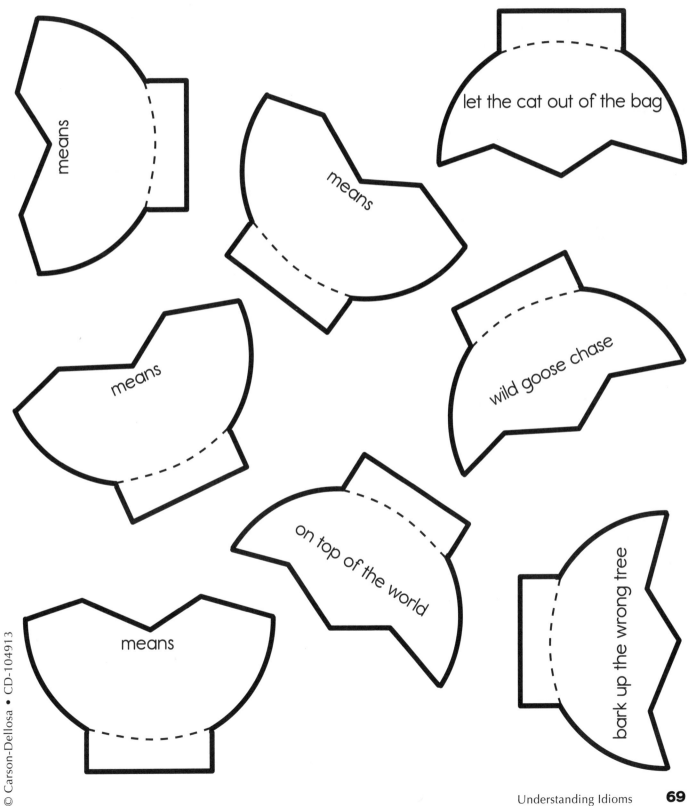

let the cat out of the bag

means

means

wild goose chase

means

on top of the world

means

bark up the wrong tree

Personification

Introduction

Remind students that personification is a figure of speech in which an idea, object, or animal is given human characteristics. Write the verbs *coughs* and *sputters* on the board. Ask students to demonstrate coughing and sputtering. Then, have students write a sentence with *The old car* as the subject, giving the car the human characteristics of coughing and sputtering. Repeat the activity with other subjects and words such as *tired*, *danced*, and *shivered*.

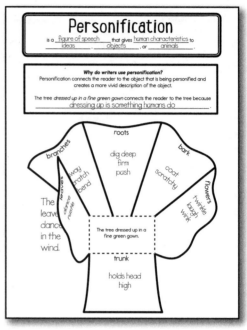

Creating the Notebook Page

Guide students through the following steps to complete the right-hand page in their notebooks.

1. Add a Table of Contents entry for the Personification pages.

2. Cut out the title and glue it to the top of the page.

3. Complete the definition of *personification* (is a **figure of speech** that gives **human characteristics** to **ideas**, **objects**, or **animals**).

4. Cut out the *Why do writers* piece. Discuss reasons that writers use personification and what it means to *connect the reader to the object being personified*. Complete the sentence. (*The tree dressed up in a fine green gown* connects the reader to the tree because ***dressing up is something that humans do.***)

5. Cut out the tree flap book. Cut on the solid lines to create six flaps. Apply glue to the back of the center section and attach it to the page. Discuss ways to give human characteristics to *leaves, branches, roots, bark, trunk,* and *flowers*. Write notes on the flaps. Under each flap, write a sentence that personifies that part of the tree.

Reflect on Learning

To complete the left-hand page, have students use the sentences they wrote under the flaps to write a poem about the tree.

Answer Key
Answers will vary but may include: The leaves dance merrily in the wind. The branches point up to the sky. The roots push their way into the earth. The bark wears a brown, scratchy coat. The trunk holds the branches above its head. The flowers wink their bright eyes.

Personification

is a _____ _____ _____ that gives _____ _____ to _____ , _____ , or _____ .

Why do writers use personification?
Personification connects the reader to the object that is being personified and creates a more vivid description of the object.

The tree *dressed up in a fine green gown* connects the reader to the tree because
_____ .

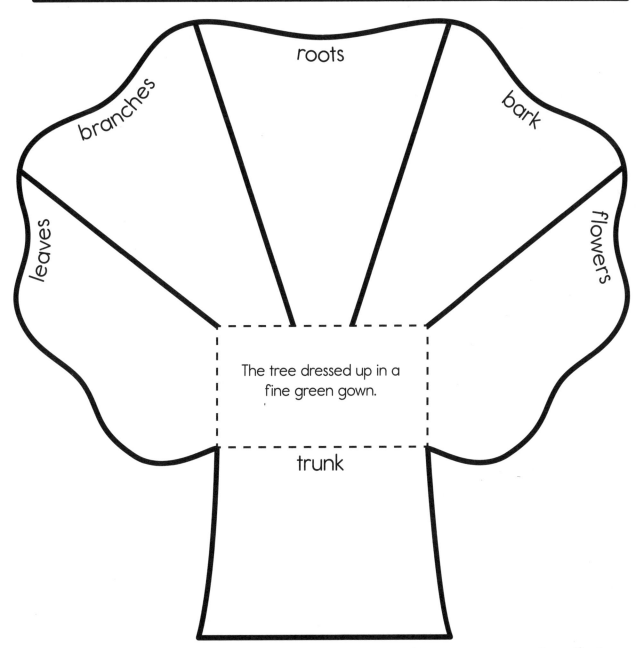

roots

branches

bark

leaves

flowers

The tree dressed up in a fine green gown.

trunk

Greek and Latin Roots

Introduction

Remind students that a root is the part of the word that carries meaning. Roots usually originate from a different language, often Greek or Latin. Discuss how learning to identify common roots can help you figure out the meaning of unfamiliar words. Divide students into three groups. Assign each group a root, such as *doc*, *spec*, and *vid*. Set a timer for two minutes. Have groups brainstorm as many words as they can that derive from their assigned root. Have students compare their list of words with other groups.

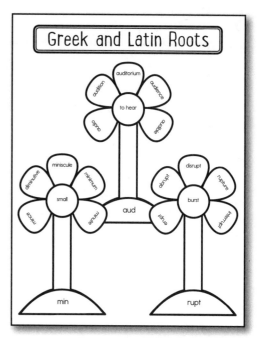

Creating the Notebook Page

Guide students through the following steps to complete the right-hand page in their notebooks.

1. Add a Table of Contents entry for the Greek and Latin Roots pages.

2. Cut out the title and glue it to the top of the page.

3. Cut out the flower stem pieces and glue them on the page in a triangle formation.

4. Cut out the *min, rupt,* and *aud* root pieces and glue them to the root sections of the flower stem pieces.

5. Cut out the word petals. Read the word on each petal and identify the root. Apply glue to the back of each petal and attach it around the correct flower center.

6. Read and think about the words that have the same root. Determine the meaning of the root.

7. Cut out the *to hear, small,* and *burst* circles. Glue each circle on the center of the flower to show the correct meaning of the root.

8. As you encounter new words with the *min, rupt,* or *aud* roots, revisit the page and add the words by drawing new petals on the flowers.

Reflect on Learning

To complete the left-hand page, have students write a sentence for each word on the flower petals.

Answer Key
aud: audition, audience, audio, audible, auditorium; min: minimum, diminutive, miniscule, mince, minute; rupt: rupture, erupt, disrupt, abrupt, interrupt

Greek and Latin Roots

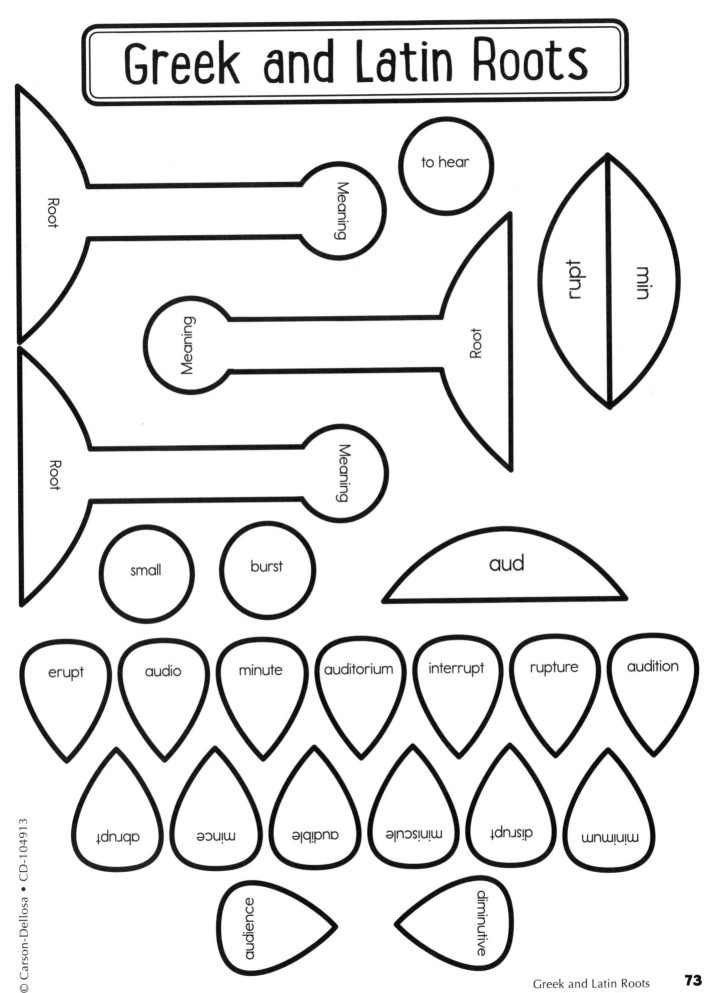

to hear

Meaning

Root

rupt | min

Meaning

Root

Meaning

Root

small   burst   aud

erupt   audio   minute   auditorium   interrupt   rupture   audition

abrupt   mince   audible   miniscule   disrupt   minimum

audience   diminutive

Using Reference Materials

Introduction

Before the lesson, gather one copy of each of the following reference materials: almanac, atlas, dictionary, encyclopedia, glossary, and thesaurus. Remind students that reference materials help us find information. Divide students into six groups. Assign each group one of the reference sources. Discuss the purpose of each one. Then, have groups make a list of the kinds of information that can be found in their assigned reference source. Provide time for students to share their lists.

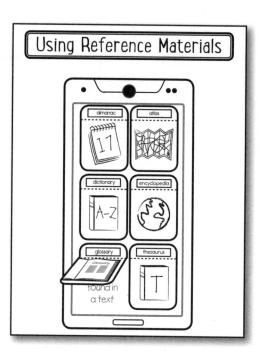

Creating the Notebook Page

Guide students through the following steps to complete the right-hand page in their notebooks.

1. Add a Table of Contents entry for the Using Reference Materials pages.

2. Cut out the title and glue it to the top of the page.

3. Cut out the smart phone piece and glue it to the page.

4. Cut out the app flaps. Apply glue to the back of the top section of each flap and attach them to the smart phone in a 2 by 3 grid.

5. Cut out the reference material labels and glue each one on top of an app flap.

6. Design and draw an app icon for each reference material on the outside of the flap.

7. Write a brief description of each reference material under the corresponding flap.

Reflect on Learning

To complete the left-hand page, have students write a brief opinion piece about their preferences of print versus online reference materials.

Answer Key
Answers will vary but may include: almanac: lists facts and statistics, is published yearly; atlas: includes maps, shows map keys and scale; dictionary: lists meaning and pronunciation of words, shows guide words, tells part of speech; encyclopedia: lists different topics alphabetically, may include pictures and diagrams; glossary: lists and defines words found in a specific text; thesaurus: includes synonyms and antonyms for words

Using Reference Materials

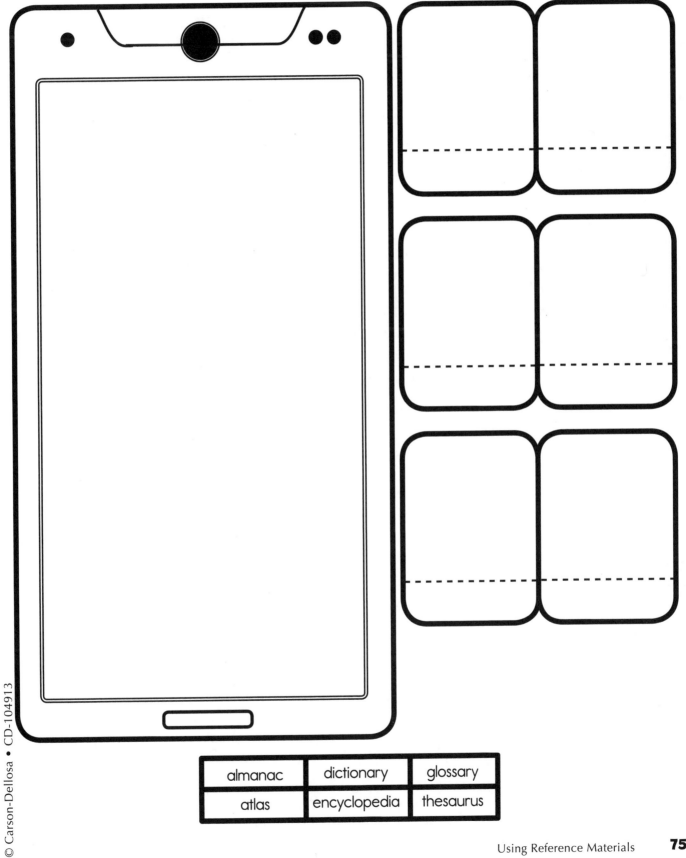

almanac	dictionary	glossary
atlas	encyclopedia	thesaurus

Understanding Analogies

Introduction

Before class, prepare three brown bags, each containing two objects: a piece of chalk and a picture of a chalkboard; a rock and a feather; a small lid and a jar. Divide the class into three groups, giving each group a bag. Have groups brainstorm ways the objects are related. Tell students that an analogy is a comparison of two words that are related in some way. Understanding word relationships helps build and strengthen vocabulary. Explain that some analogies show purpose: chalk is used to write on a chalkboard; some show synonyms or antonyms: a rock is heavy and feather is light; and some show a part to a whole: a lid is a part of a jar. Have groups write other analogies that belong to these three categories.

Understanding Analogies

synonym/antonym	toss is to throw as leap is to	? jump
	graceful is to clumsy as asleep is to	?
	safe is to dangerous as over is to	?
part to whole	wave is to ocean as leaf is to	?
	city is to state as state is to	?
	finger is to hand as petal is to	?
purpose	clue is to mystery as key is	?
	clock is to time as ruler is to	? ngth
	scissors are to cut as fork is to	?

Purpose Analogy:
glasses are to read as boots are to hike

Creating the Notebook Page

Guide students through the following steps to complete the right-hand page in their notebooks.

1. Add a Table of Contents entry for the Understanding Analogies pages.

2. Cut out the title and glue it to the top of the page.

3. Cut out the analogies flap book. Cut on the solid lines to create nine flaps. Apply glue to the back of the entire left section and attach it below the title.

4. Read each analogy. Discuss the relationship between the first two words being compared in each section. Complete the analogy by writing a word under the question mark flap.

5. Discuss the three different sets of analogies and how the three analogies in each set are alike. Cut out the *purpose, part to whole,* and *synonym/antonym* labels. Glue each label along the left side of the page to identify the category for each set of analogies.

6. Below the flap, write one more analogy and label the category.

Reflect on Learning

To complete the left-hand page, have students write a sentence to describe the relationships of each of the analogies. For example, *We use a clock to measure time in the same way that we use a ruler to measure length.*

Answer Key
Synonyms/Antonyms: toss is to throw as leap is to jump, graceful is to clumsy as awake is to asleep, safe is to dangerous as over is to under; Part to Whole: wave is to ocean as leaf is to tree, city is to state as state is to country, finger is to hand as petal is to flower; Purpose: clue is to mystery as key is to door, clock is to time as ruler is to length, scissors is to cut as fork is to eat

Understanding Analogies

toss is to throw as leap is to	**?**
graceful is to clumsy as asleep is to	**?**
safe is to dangerous as over is to	**?**
wave is to ocean as leaf is to	**?**
city is to state as state is to	**?**
finger is to hand as petal is to	**?**
clue is to mystery as key is	**?**
clock is to time as ruler is to	**?**
scissors are to cut as fork is to	**?**

Tabs

Cut out each tab and label it. Apply glue to the back of each tab and align it on the outside edge of the page with only the label section showing beyond the edge. Then, fold each tab to seal the page inside.

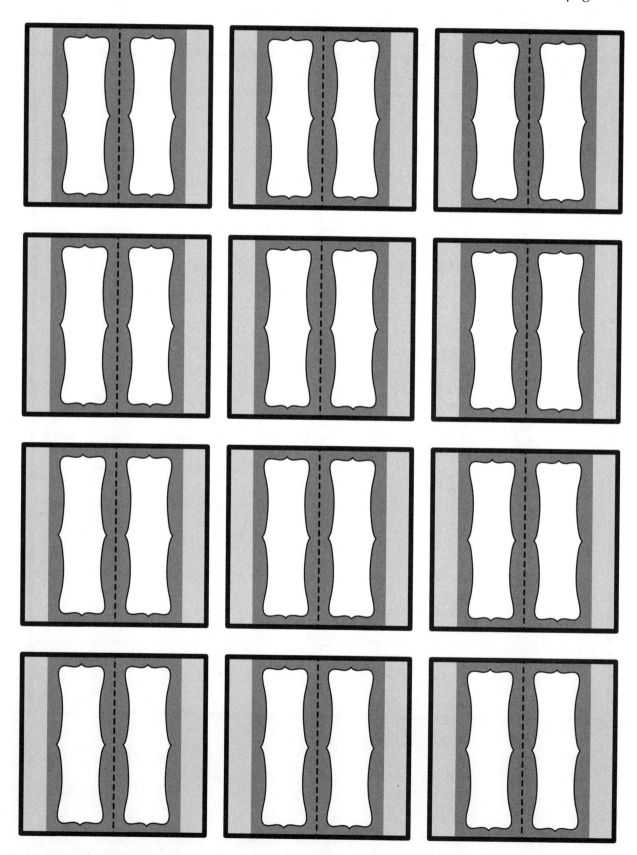

KWL Chart

Cut out the KWL chart and cut on the solid lines to create three separate flaps. Apply glue to the back of the Topic section to attach the chart to a notebook page.

What I

Know

What I

Wonder

What I

Learned

Topic:

© Carson-Dellosa • CD-104913

79

Library Pocket

Cut out the library pocket on the solid lines. Fold in the side tabs and apply glue to them before folding up the front of the pocket. Apply glue to the back of the pocket to attach it to a notebook page.

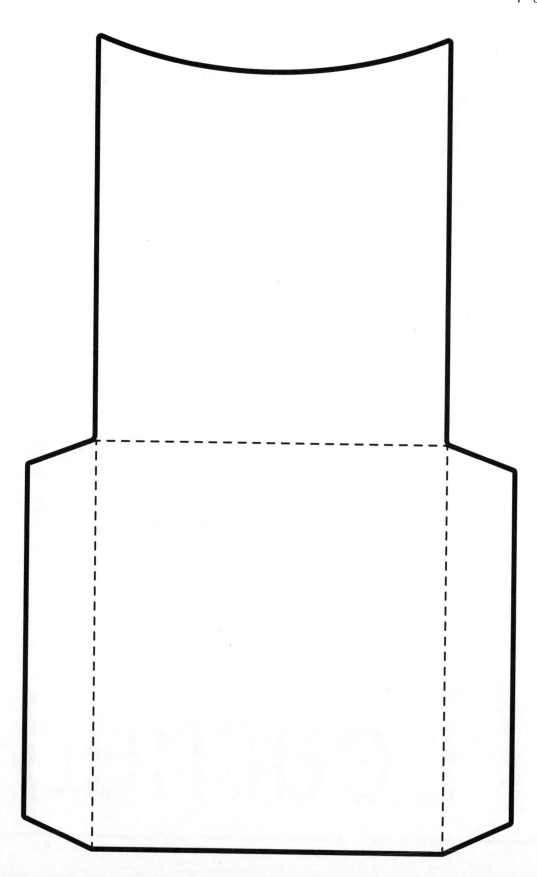

Envelope

Cut out the envelope on the solid lines. Fold in the side tabs and apply glue to them before folding up the rectangular front of the envelope. Fold down the triangular flap to close the envelope. Apply glue to the back of the envelope to attach it to a notebook page.

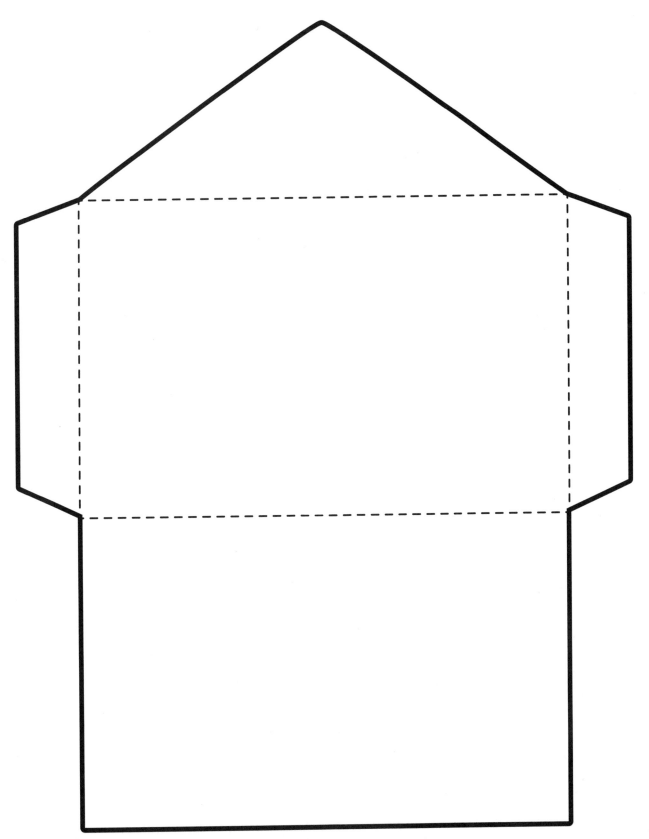

Pocket and Cards

Cut out the pocket on the solid lines. Fold over the front of the pocket. Then, apply glue to the tabs and fold them around the back of the pocket. Apply glue to the back of the pocket to attach it to a notebook page. Cut out the cards and store them in the envelope.

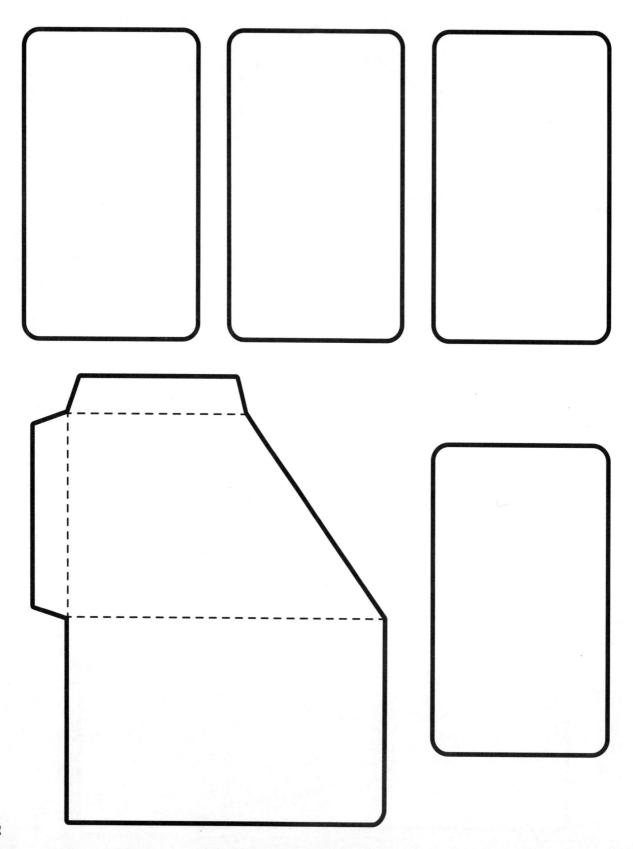

Six-Flap Shutter Fold

Cut out the shutter fold around the outside border. Then, cut on the solid lines to create six flaps. Fold the flaps toward the center. Apply glue to the back of the shutter fold to attach it to a notebook page.

If desired, this template can be modified to create a four-flap shutter fold by cutting off the bottom row. You can also create two three-flap books by cutting it in half down the center line.

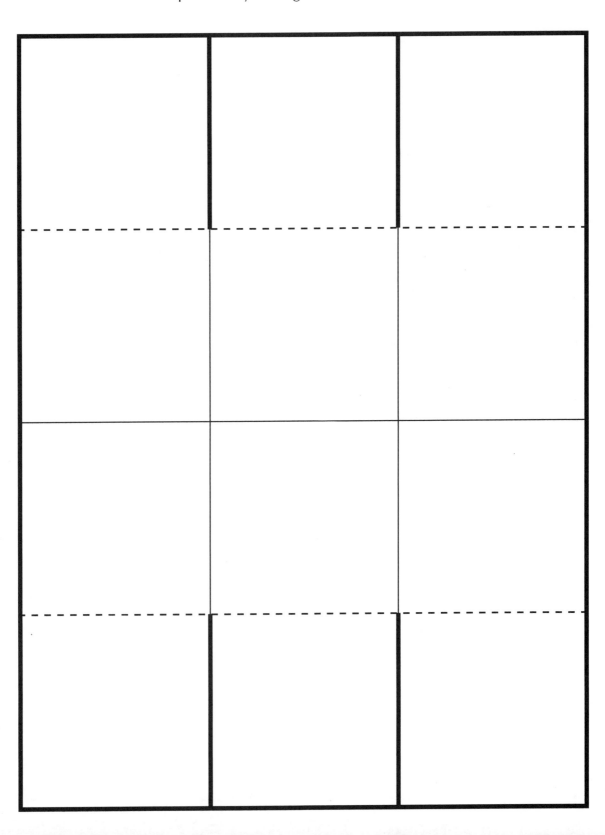

Eight-Flap Shutter Fold

Cut out the shutter fold around the outside border. Then, cut on the solid lines to create eight flaps. Fold the flaps toward the center. Apply glue to the back of the shutter fold to attach it to a notebook page.

If desired, this template can be modified to create two four-flap shutter folds by cutting off the bottom two rows. You can also create two four-flap books by cutting it in half down the center line.

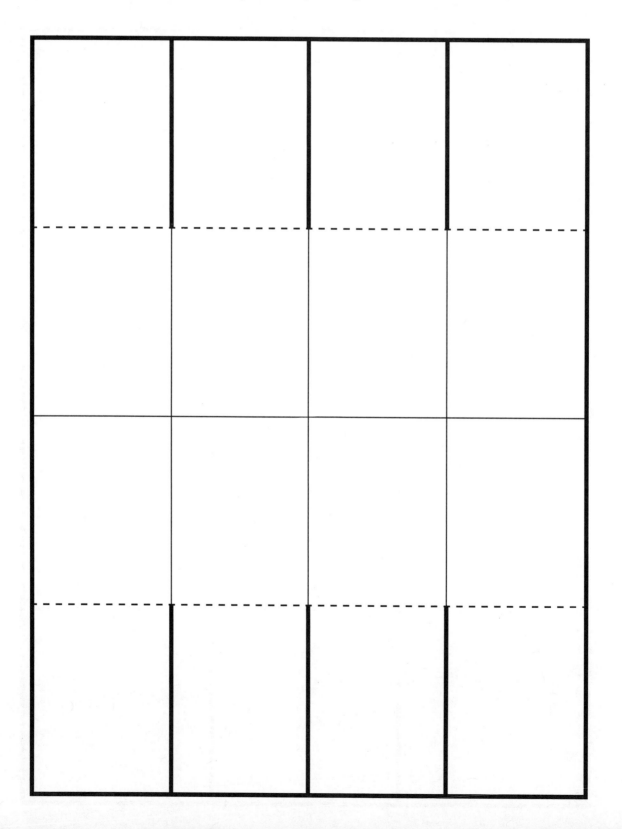

Flap Book—Eight Flaps

Cut out the flap book around the outside border. Then, cut on the solid lines to create eight flaps. Apply glue to the back of the center section to attach it to a notebook page.

If desired, this template can be modified to create a six-flap or two four-flap books by cutting off the bottom row or two. You can also create a tall four-flap book by cutting off the flaps on the left side.

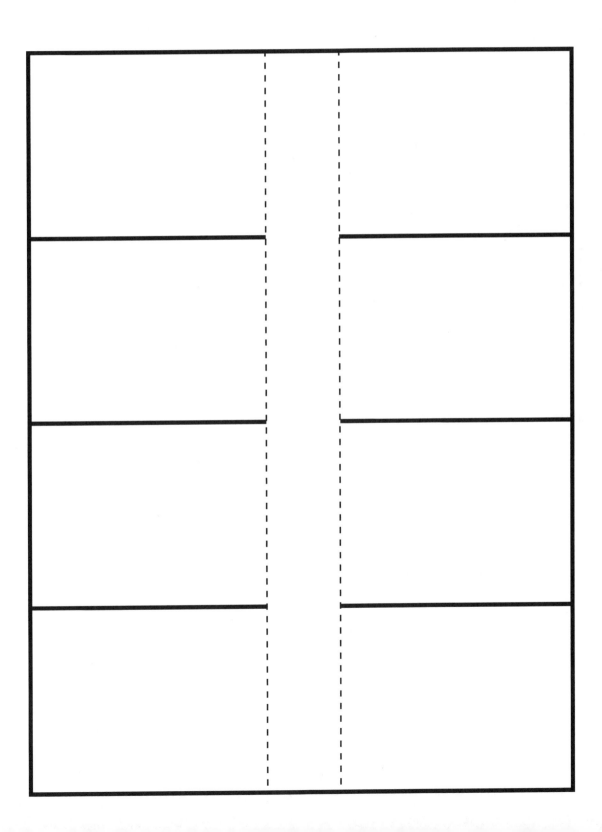

Flap Book—Twelve Flaps

Cut out the flap book around the outside border. Then, cut on the solid lines to create 12 flaps. Apply glue to the back of the center section to attach it to a notebook page.

If desired, this template can be modified to create smaller flap books by cutting off any number of rows from the bottom. You can also create a tall flap book by cutting off the flaps on the left side.

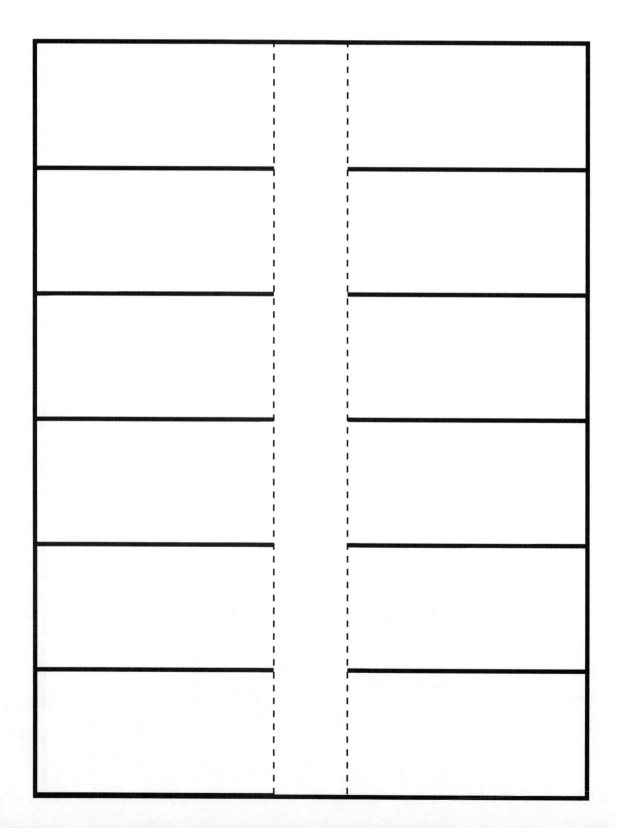

Shaped Flaps

Cut out each shaped flap. Apply glue to the back of the narrow section to attach it to a notebook page.

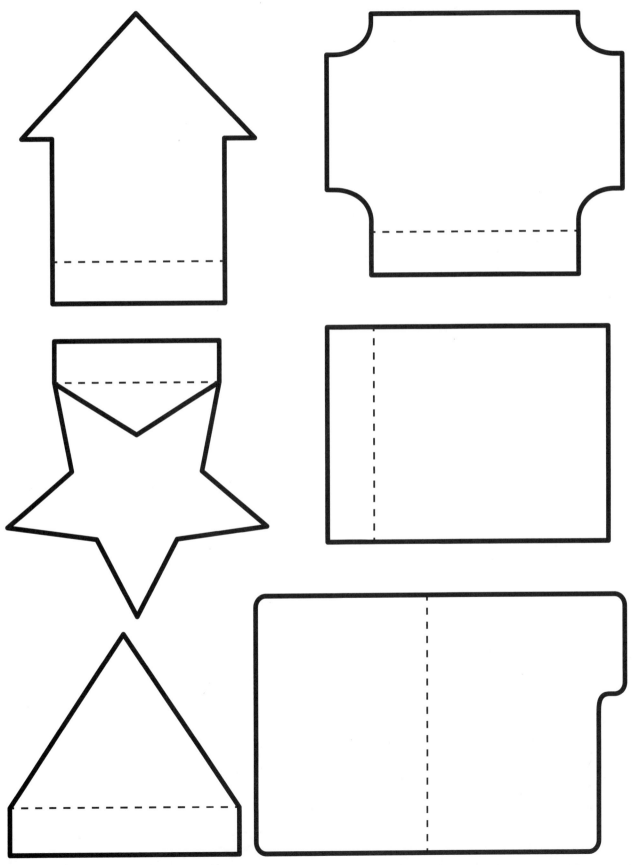

Shaped Flaps

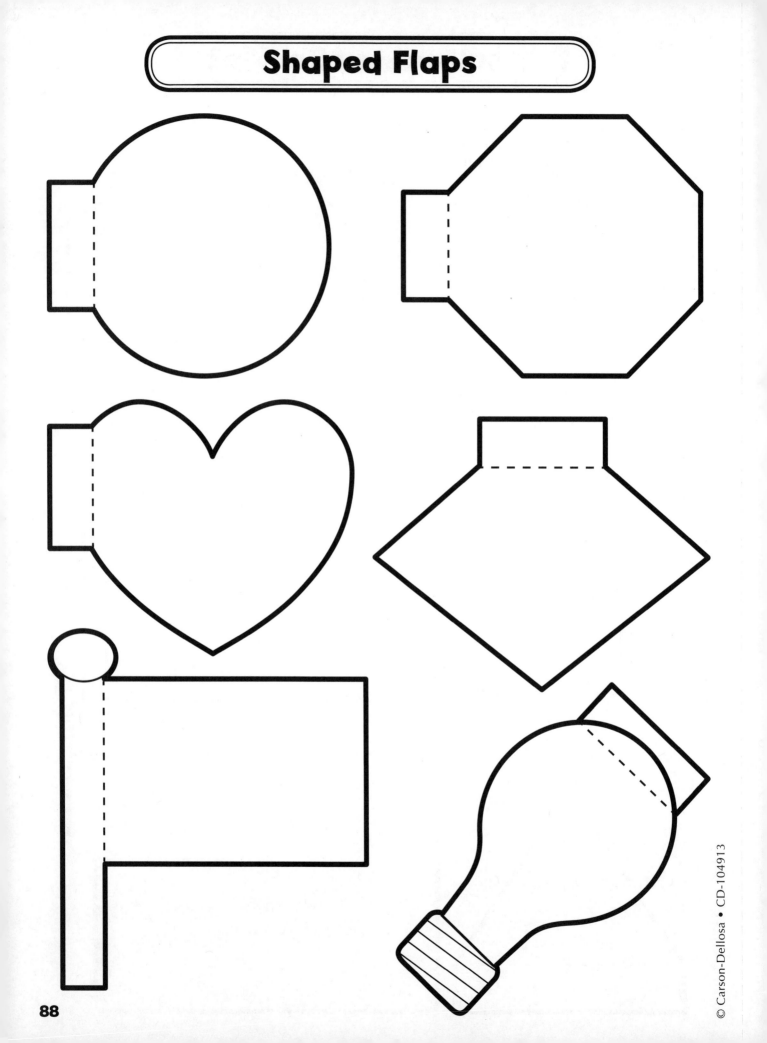

Interlocking Booklet

Cut out the booklet on the solid lines, including the short vertical lines on the top and bottom flaps. Then, fold the top and bottom flaps toward the center, interlocking them using the small vertical cuts. Apply glue to the back of the center panel to attach it to a notebook page.

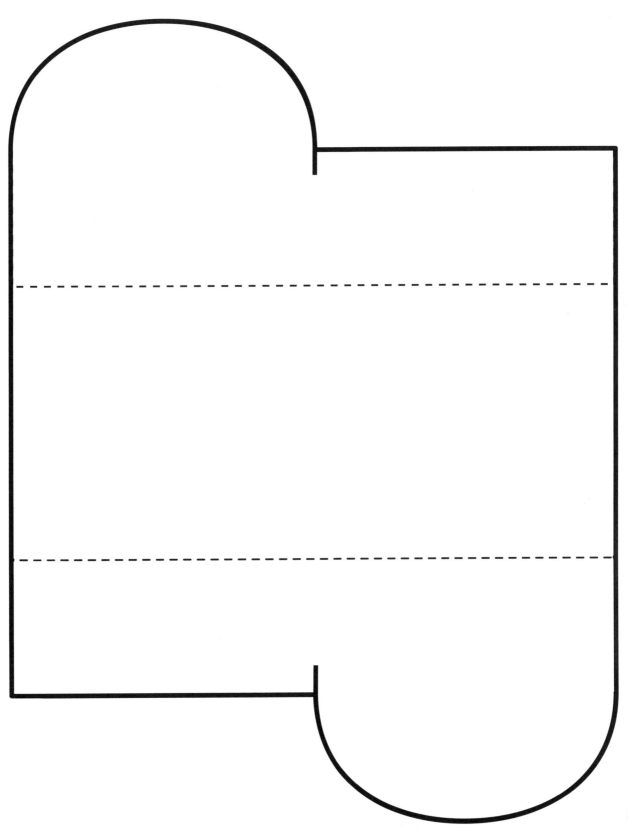

Four-Flap Petal Fold

Cut out the shape on the solid lines. Then, fold the flaps toward the center. Apply glue to the back of the center panel to attach it to a notebook page.

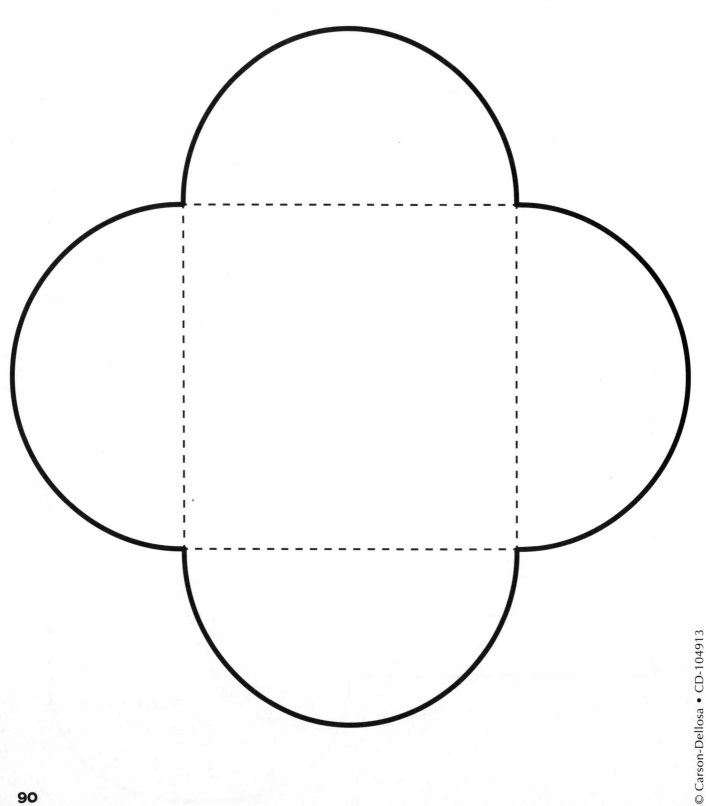

Six-Flap Petal Fold

Cut out the shape on the solid lines. Then, fold the flaps toward the center and back out. Apply glue to the back of the center panel to attach it to a notebook page.

Accordion Folds

Cut out the accordion pieces on the solid lines. Fold on the dashed lines, alternating the fold direction. Apply glue to the back of the last section to attach it to a notebook page.

You may modify the accordion books to have more or fewer pages by cutting off extra pages or by having students glue the first and last panels of two accordion books together.

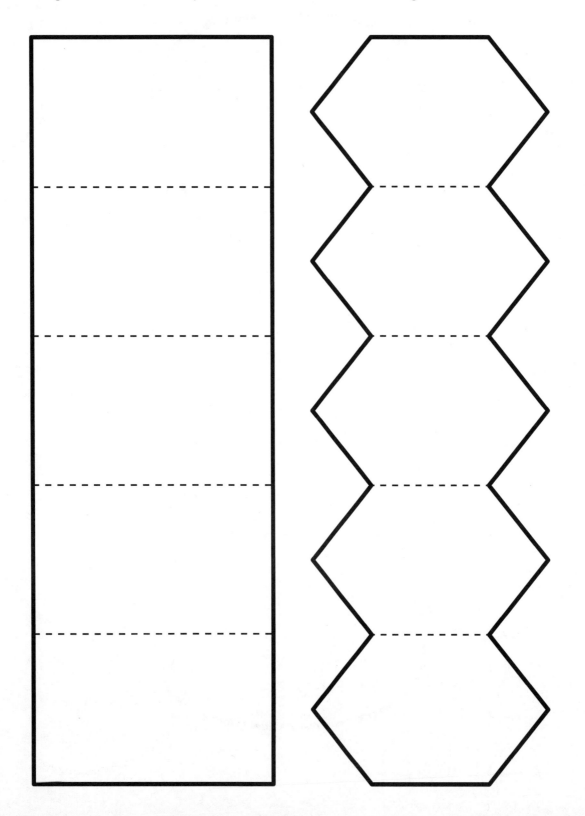

92

Accordion Folds

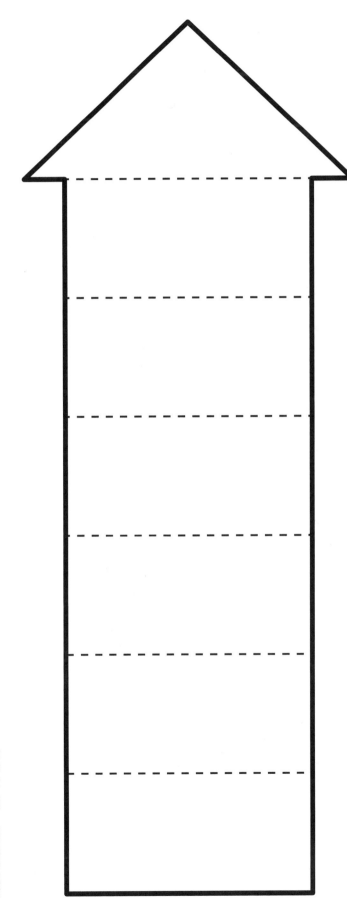

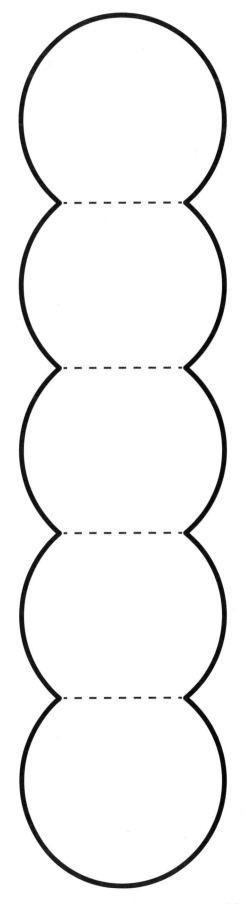

Clamshell Fold

Cut out the clamshell fold on the solid lines. Fold and unfold the piece on the three dashed lines. With the piece oriented so that the folds form an X with a horizontal line through it, pull the left and right sides together at the fold line. Then, keeping the sides touching, bring the top edge down to meet the bottom edge. You should be left with a triangular shape that unfolds into a square. Apply glue to the back of the triangle to attach the clamshell to a notebook page.

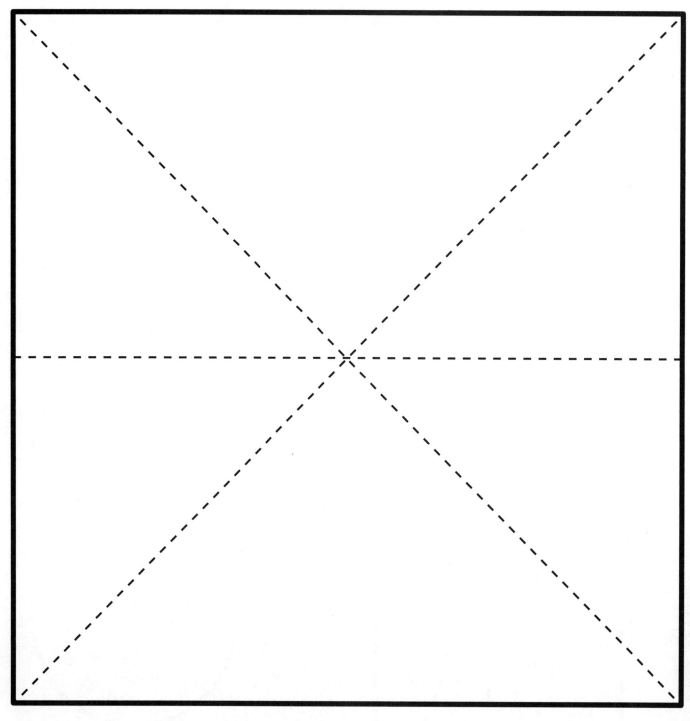

94

Puzzle Pieces

Cut out each puzzle along the solid lines to create a three- or four-piece puzzle. Apply glue to the back of each puzzle piece to attach it to a notebook page. Alternately, apply glue only to one edge of each piece to create flaps.

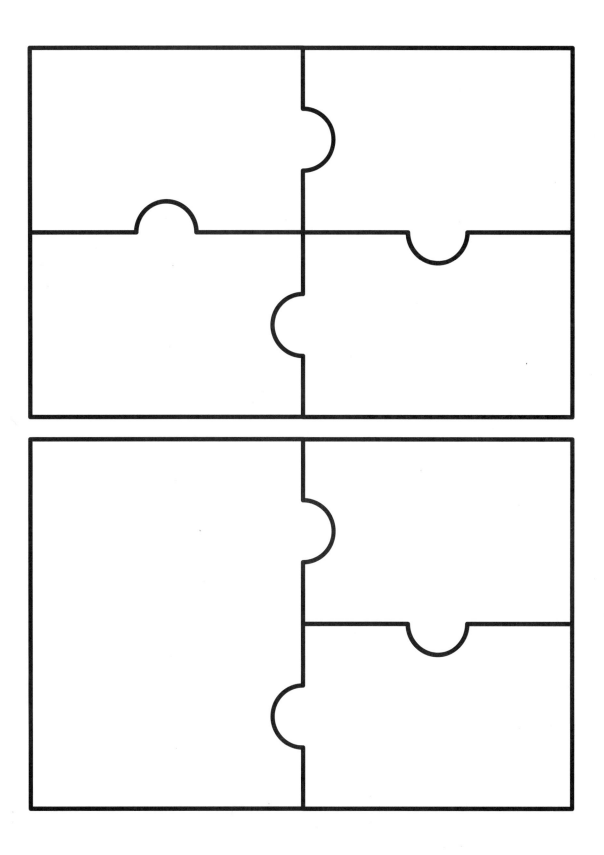

Flip Book

Cut out the two rectangular pieces on the solid lines. Fold each rectangle on the dashed lines. Fold the piece with the gray glue section so that it is inside the fold. Apply glue to the gray glue section and place the other folded rectangle on top so that the folds are nested and create a book with four cascading flaps. Make sure that the inside pages are facing up so that the edges of both pages are visible. Apply glue to the back of the book to attach it to a notebook page.

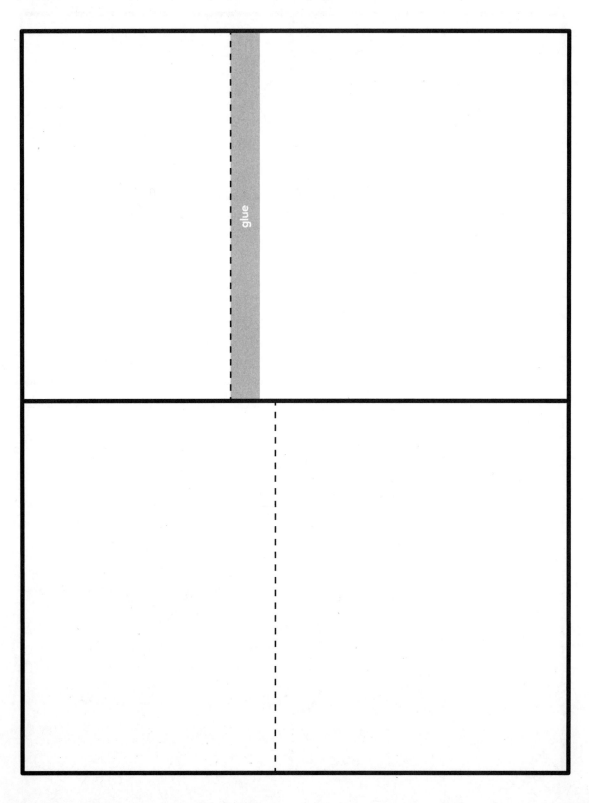

glue